THE NEW
MEDITERRANEAN
INSTANT POT
COOKBOOK

Eva Evans

LEGAL & DISCLAIMER

The information contained in this book and its contents is not designed to replace or take the place of any form of medical or professional advice; and is not meant to replace the need for independent medical, financial, legal, or other professional advice or services, as may be required. The content and information in this book has been provided for educational and entertainment purposes only.

The content and information contained in this book has been compiled from sources deemed reliable, and it is accurate to the best of the Author's knowledge, information, and belief. However, the Author cannot guarantee its accuracy and validity and cannot be held liable for any errors and/or omissions. Further, changes are periodically made to this book as and when needed. Where appropriate and/or necessary, you must consult a professional (including but not limited to your doctor, attorney, financial advisor, or such other professional advisor) before using any of the suggested remedies, techniques, or information in this book.

Upon using the contents and information contained in this book, you agree to hold harmless the Author from and against any damages, costs, and expenses, including any legal fees potentially resulting from the application of any of the information provided by this book. This disclaimer applies to any loss, damages or injury caused by the use and application, whether directly or indirectly, of any advice or information presented, whether for breach of contract, tort, negligence, personal injury, criminal intent, or under any other cause of action. You agree to accept all risks of using the information presented inside this book. You agree that by continuing to read this book, where appropriate and/or necessary, you shall consult a professional (including but not limited to your doctor, attorney, or financial advisor or such other advisor as needed) before using any of the suggested remedies, techniques, or information in this book.

TABLE OF CONTENT

INTRODUCTION

Based on the diets from the southern European countries such as Italy, Greece, and Crete, the Mediterranean diet is not only one of the most delicious, but one of the healthiest as well.

People in these countries tend to have good health, slender bodies (no matter how much they eat) and live long and quality life.

Of course, there are many factors for that (such as nature and genes), but in general, the food you are consuming plays the largest role in the way how you feel, look, and how healthy you would be.

The Mediterranean diet mainly offers whole grains, fresh fruits and vegetables, good fats (fish, olive oil, nuts), fish, and a very small amount of other types of meat.

But, it is not only the food you are consuming but also how you do that. People these days have less time to sit down and enjoy their meals let alone gather the family and enjoy their lunch or dinner for a longer time.

Combined with a proper physical activity, this diet also provides the best results – healthy and fit body, good mood, and above all, feeling excellent in your skin.

The Mediterranean diet is a lifestyle, a form of self-love. Not only it would help you lose the extra weight, but it would do miracles for your internal organs, and general health.

6

Unlike any other diet, this is a diet you can follow for as long as you wish. It is not harsh to switch to it, and would certainly keep you fAull after every meal.

Natural slimming, while eating delicious foods (fresh above all) is the ideal way of losing weight. There are no extended periods of starving, you will not retrain yourself from delicious meals, nor will you feel moody because you are hungry. If your goal is losing weight without gaining it back, and become healthier, I would love to discuss this diet with you.

The Mediterranean Diet is an eating pattern that will bring a healthy change in your eating habits.

Enjoying food and looking forward to the next meal is crucial in this diet. I am sure that everybody who tries this diet would enjoy the meals.

What is important is that it is rich in healthy, yet delicious foods. That is what makes it popular and loved.

Starting this diet will help you become more mindful of the foods you are eating, how fresh they are, and the ingredients they have.

Mindful eating is the most important step that would lead you on the way of becoming a healthier, fitter, and happier person.

This book's goal is to initiate you and take you through the process of starting the Mediterranean diet. Together, we will learn about why it so good for your health, if you could actually slim with it and what foods are great for you.

Without further ado, let's dive into the first chapter.

HOW DOES MEDITERRANEAN DIET WORK?

Recognized by the UN as an endangered species, this diet, or rather an eating pattern, is based on the eating habits of rural people, who mainly ate what they grew. These people did not have the money to buy expensive foods (back in the days expensive food was meat), so they were mainly focused on eating the things they were able to pick from the ground and trees, or foods they were able to produce on their own such as pasta, oils, or catch in the sea (seafood).

In 2013, UNESCO listed this diet as part of the cultural heritage of countries around the Mediterranean, such as Greece, Italy, Spain, Morocco, Portugal, Croatia, and Cyprus.

In the beginning, I want to point out that by starting this diet, you will not magically and suddenly transform into a slender person without cholesterol issues.

Nothing happens overnight, but if you follow it regularly, this diet could help you lower the risk of heart and blood vessel illnesses by about 25%.

People who live in Mediterranean countries are known to be healthy, slender, and live longer. We cannot say the same for people who live fast-paced lives, eat junk and fast food, do not work out, and are exposed to stress every single day.

Don't get me wrong – people from the Mediterranean countries are not immune to diseases like heart attacks or cancer, but the risk of getting these illnesses is significantly lower.

The first thing you think about the Mediterranean is an amazing nature, great food, delicious wine, sunny days, and people who are friendly and content with their lives.

What is the secret for Mediterranean people being healthier and slender?

The answer is simple - they eat plenty of fresh and whole food. Fruits and vegetables are always on their menu. You would agree that some of the most delicious Mediterranean meals are so simple and have nothing else but vegetables and olive oil.

Eating a diet based on fruits, vegetables, fish, nuts, and healthy oils, would make your body detox from all the artificial ingredients you stocked while eating junk and fast food. Providing your body with healthy nutrients, vitamins, minerals, proteins, healthy fats, and a reasonable amount in carbohydrates would lead to an easy slimming. Also, you would reduce the risk of getting diabetes, cholesterol, heart failures, and cancer. The Mediterranean Diet is focused on whole-grain foods, healthy fats (olive oil, nuts, fish), fruits, vegetables, and small amounts of red meat (consumed rarely). So, how does it work?

The crucial thing about this diet is that it encourages you to cook your food, pay attention to it, dine with your family, and actually slow down when you consume your meal. This way, you pay attention to the flavors and how your food is cooked.

Of course, you can do this with any diet, but this diet has no processed food at all. Nothing contains added sugars or other ingredients to keep the food fresher for a longer time.

Your meals contain fresh and whole fruits and vegetables (picked from the tree and ground and delivered to your table). Also, you would consume lean meats like fish, olive oil, whole grains, and legumes and almost no processed food and sweets.

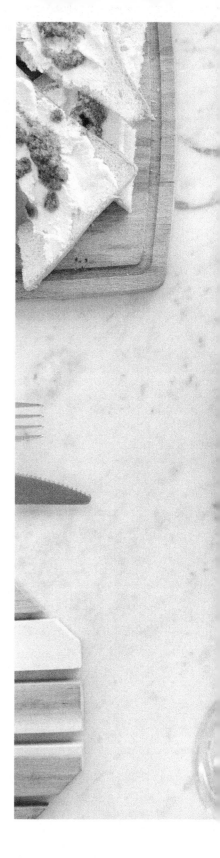

Providing your body with such quality ingredients would help it get what it needs, without making reserves of fats that will not be used. When consuming unhealthy foods rich in fats and carbs, your body uses the energy from the carbs, and the fats are stored (which is why there are layers of fat around your stomach, arms, and legs).

With a clean and healthy diet, your body gets to use the healthy ingredients, and to burn the fats (since there are no high amounts of carbs in your diet, your body seeks the second best energy source, which is the fat).

If you decide to start exercising, your diet will show even better results.

The most important thing, I believe you would love, is that this diet is not encouraging you to starve or skip meals. Every meal is important, and every meal must contain healthy ingredients.

You would start your day with a light breakfast. Sure, the light meal will not keep you full for a long time, so instead of going for a snack, you should get a piece of fruit such as berries, a banana, pear, or whatever fruit you like.

Your lunch is the next meal that includes plenty of vegetables combined with healthy fats such as olive oil, cheese, and nuts, and you would finish your day with a dish that contains fish and vegetables, and a glass of red wine.

Following this diet will not stop you from eating foods that have carbohydrates. In this diet, carbs are welcomed. After all, those delicious pasta dishes combined with cooked sauce are people's favorite.

Carbohydrates are not your enemy if they are consumed in the right amount and combined with healthy fats (seafood, fish, olive oil), and vegetables. They are only bad for your weight if it is the only thing you are eating and in large amounts without providing your body with healthy fats, proteins, vitamins, and minerals.

As I mentioned, a large amount of carbs helps the body focus on burning the carbs only so it can crate glucose which is the brains' main energy source.

The good thing about this diet is that it is so abundant, you can pick any recipe you want from French, Italian, Spanish, or Greek cuisine.

Also, you have already noticed I used the phrase eating pattern instead of a diet. It is because you are not restraining yourself from anything but high amounts of processed and junk food, and you get to eat clean, delicious, and healthy foods. It is more a pattern, which gives you the right to pick what foods you would eat and how many calories you would consume daily.

There is the so-called Mediterranean diet pyramid that would help you learn how to start and create your initial meal plan.

This pyramid's main focus is daily eating of vegetables, fruits, whole grains, nuts, olive oil, fish, seafood, beans, and legumes. These foods should be present in your menu at least five times a week.

Eggs, cheese, poultry, and yogurt should be consumed in lesser amounts, while sweets, soda drinks, heavy liquor, and red meat should be consumed rarely.

So, nothing is forbidden; there are only foods that should be your main go-to ingredients and foods that should be eaten only occasionally.

Perhaps you do not want to give up on alcohol, but this eating pattern allows red wine (in moderate amounts). One glass of red wine for women and two for men; if you are not a fan of wine, it is not a mandatory drink, of course.

So, if you are about to try this eating pattern because you want results overnight, I would have to break it down to you and disappoint you. You will have to be patient before you see results. The best way to slim down is to do it gradually over weeks and even months.One thing I can say for sure is that people tend to overeat when they are bored or alone when they have fast food within the reach in their desk or at home.

People constantly feel hunger even after eating a huge amount of calories. That is because you are only satisfying your flavor buds and not providing your body with what it needs. Junk food is packed in flavors that feel good and make you feel content. But, the results, in the long run, are not only obesity but health issues as well.So, what are the foods you should put on your list before starting this diet? Let's check in the following chapter.

15

DO I HAVE THE RIGHT INGREDIENTS TO START THIS DIET?

Now that you decided to start this eating pattern, you would have to get the ingredients.

There is no big philosophy here. You are allowed to get your favorite fruits, vegetables, seeds, nuts, and anything that grows in the garden.

This is not a vegan or vegetarian diet since you are allowed to eat fish and seafood, and occasionally red meat.

Fish and seafood should be on your table a few times a week.

When it comes to dairy food, it should be consumed in moderation, just like red meat.

Red wine is the drink you can always go to if you feel like having some alcohol. However, you should not drink it too often or in large amounts. A glass of red wine with your meal is more than enough.

Keep in mind that your food should be fresh (at least twice a day you should eat fruits and vegetables). Also, if you want to follow the proper Mediterranean diet, you would have to start taking your meals seriously. This means, your meals should be cooked and enjoyed in peace without rushing.

Resting after a meal is very important. Most people cannot afford to rest after a meal, but if you have the chance to slow down a little bit and let your stomach digest your meal, do it without hesitation.

I would like to point out that this is not a harsh diet that will make you feel hungry; you will always have delicious meals on your menu. So, even if you decide to change your eating habits drastically, you will feel that something is missing on your plate.

What people love about it is that they do not have to accommodate to new foods. We have all tried tomatoes, fish, apples, watermelons, onions, garlic, olive oil.

Your body would not be stressed out by any new flavors. Your only challenge would be to adapt to a healthier lifestyle and end the habit of consuming sugary and processed foods. Allow yourself to take the time and transit to your menu slowly.

Here Are The Foods You Can Eat In This Diet.

I am sure you already have a bottle of *extra-virgin olive* oil at home. If not, now is the time to get one. Sure, you can cook with butter and any other oil, but it will mess up your diet and would not provide you with the healthy fats you need. Extra-virgin olive oil is great for fresh salads, cooking fish and seafood.

Provide your kitchen with *nuts and seeds*. Your regular processed snacks are not welcome in this diet. Instead, you would go for a healthy substitute. Start with pumpkin seeds, hazelnuts, walnuts, chia seeds, chickpeas, corn, or cashews.

You can combine them in your breakfasts, snacks, desserts, and even your dinner. They are rich in iron and proteins and will suppress your hunger in between meals.

Next, you should get *fish and seafood*. Some people are not fans of seafood; you can always start slowly. Red meat is not your friend. It is responsible for high cholesterol and triglycerides. Meat is not adding to your weight if eaten moderately. If consumed every day with a large number of carbohydrates like French fries and white bread, it would add weight and put your health at risk.

Your body needs the omega-3 fatty acids that are healthy and help you slim easily. Fish and seafood are the best foods for your health.

Known for its properties when it comes to improving your sight, strengthening your hair and nails, and lower the risk of heart failures, seafood and fish should be consumed at least twice a week. Omega-3 fatty acids work as an anti-inflammatory agent and are an excellent nutrient that helps in boosting your immunity but also in fighting depression and anxiety.

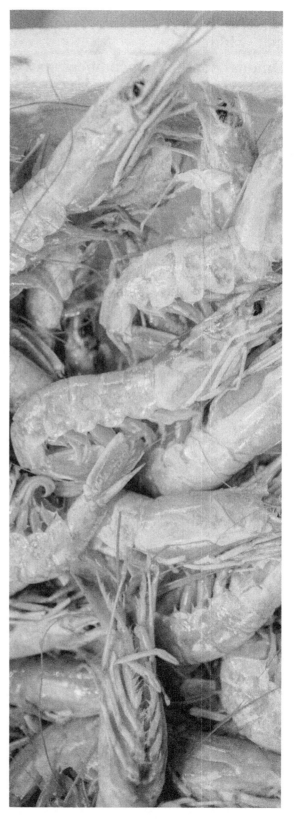

Of course, you cannot begin this diet without *fruits and veggies*. Onions, garlic, cucumber, peas, potatoes, zucchini, green beans, mushrooms, broccoli, you name it. Also, leafy greens like spinach, kale, lettuce should be on your menu. They are great for salads, pasta, and side dish.

When it comes to fruit, go for your favorites; you cannot make a mistake with seasonal fruits like apples, bananas, or berries. Fruits are wonderful as snacks, but also as breakfast ingredients (combine them occasionally with Greek yogurt and oatmeal).

Beans and legumes should be on the table of every beginner. You would need lentils, beans, and chickpeas. These foods are great for your salads, but also as a side dish with your lunch or dinner.

I mentioned that *dairy products* are not recommended for everyday use, but you can still use them. Add some feta cheese, ricotta, Mozzarella, or parmesan in your breakfast, salads, or pasta.

Now, as mentioned above, this is not a diet that recommends frequent use of meat. But also, it is not a vegetarian or vegan diet, so the meat is not entirely excluded. If you do not want to give up on meat abruptly, include it once or twice a week, but in moderate amounts. *Beef and chicken* are great options.

When it comes to carbohydrates, *bread and pasta* are your friends. Sandwiches, pasta (spaghetti, macaroni, you name it) are not excluded. Just always make sure you consume bread and pasta made of whole grains.

Eggs are not excluded from this diet, so you do not have to quit them.

Although processed foods are not the best option (due to the heavy amount of added salt and sugars), *pantry food* is absolutely all right. You can use canned beans, tomatoes, corn, and chickpeas. To be sure you are consuming healthy ingredients, always read the ingredient list. Foods that have a long ingredient list are not your ideal option.

And finally, *herbs*; Mediterranean cuisines are so amazing and smell so inviting because of the herbs. Fresh cilantro, rosemary, black pepper, parsley, cumin, basil, dill, garlic, and onion should find a place in your kitchen. Of course, herbs are not mandatory, if you do not enjoy them.

The main ingredients to start the Mediterranean diet are seasonal veggies and fruits of your choice, nuts, bread, and pasta made of whole grain and fish and seafood.

23

HOW EASY IS TO FOLLOW THE MEDITERRANEAN DIET?

There is no right answer to this question. I can say it is easy for me, but for another person, it may not be the best option.

Here is why.

Some people spent their entire life eating foods like hamburgers, chips, soda drinks, processed foods and meats, and junk food. Their taste buds are used on those flavors. People who eat such foods are not necessarily unhealthy or overweight, but extended eating of such foods would take its toll in the later years of age.

Now, when a person whose diet is mainly focused on processed food tries to change it and begins to eat fresh and whole-food, they might not get used to it immediately.

Some people are not fans of fruits and vegetables and prefer eating their meat more frequently. Seafood and fish might not be everyone's favorite as well.

So it is not the food that is a problem but re-creating your old habits.

However, the good news is that transitioning into this way of eating is not a stress for your organism. Sure, you might have cravings for sweets and junk snacks, but that is normal. The body would want to have what it was used on.

So, in the beginning, you might feel like breaking your eating pattern with a giant hamburger with fries and a soda drink. But, once you allow yourself to adapt to the new meals, you would be surprised that you no longer crave anything.

The good thing about this diet is that it is not going to make you starve or eat super small dishes with foods you don't like.

From the food list in the previous chapter, you already saw that Mediterranean meals contain foods you already eat. There are no restrictions, only foods that are a priority and are consumed every day, and foods that should be consumed moderately.

Some people cannot imagine their day without a dairy product or eggs. The key lies in a slow transit. Reduce the foods you usually ate to twice or three times a week.

Don't let your brain think that something is forbidden (if you were ever on a diet, you know that the cravings are unbearable when foods are forbidden to you).

Every meal contains enough calories to keep you full, and you are allowed to eat healthy snacks (nuts, fruits, and veggies).

This is an eating pattern, and that is all you have to think of. You can combine your ingredients without counting calories. You will never be hungry, and by the end of your first week, you would be entirely used on your new meals.

Don't feel bad if you allow yourself to still eat the foods you used to eat before this diet. In fact, the best way to adapt to this diet is to start slowly.

Start with a few meals first. Instead of having your usual meat dish, substitute it with fish or seafood. See how your body reacts and if you like the taste.

Some people may find that Mediterranean meals are abundant in vegetables. Even if you love vegetables, this transition might be hard work for you. You might feel as if though you are hungry and that the vegetable stew did not satisfy your hunger.

Instead to jump for an entire vegetable meal, add a bowl of salad with your lunch or steam veggies with your chicken steak dinner.

The same goes for fruit. If you were used to eating fruit a few times a week in the past, it may be a challenge to eat two or three pieces of fruit on a daily basis. Create a habit to eat a piece of fruit every day with your breakfast or as a snack between your breakfast and lunch.

Another challenge could be to follow the diet if you tend to eat out more frequently (some people spend most of their day at work or school). You can always pick a Mediterranean meal, but when you are exposed to so many choices, you might 'fail' and go back to the foods you are now trying to avoid.

This leads us to the fact that now you will have to start cooking your meals. This might be a huge challenge for some people. Some people simply hate cooking, they do not have the time for it or are not very skilled cooks. No matter the fact that Mediterranean dishes do not require some extraordinary cooking skills, this could be a major setback for many people. If you want to still follow this diet and spend less time in the kitchen, you could cook a few meals in advance. Create your meal plan, cook, and store everything in glass containers in the freeze. Not only will you save time, but also electricity and energy.

Your first week is your best test. You would either dedicate yourself to it and see if you could last for a longer time, or you would simply give up and continue eating like before.

The most important thing is your willingness to make it. If you convince yourself that you would change your old unhealthy eating habits and you would endure it, there is no reason for you to fail.

Every transition is slow and even challenging. This is why you should test the waters first instead to dive in.

Allow yourself to get familiar with the new tastes. Let your body adjust to the new nutrients.

This is a basic eating pattern for healthy eating. If your main goal is to lose weight without starving, the Mediterranean diet is your ideal first step.

None of the ingredients is strange to you (you surly have tasted fruits and vegetables and fish before). The unhealthy foods would still be on the menu, while you are progressing towards your new ways of eating.

There is everything in this diet, from proteins to fats, bread, pasta, fruits, veggies, nuts, and even wine.

At the end of the day, you will not feel different (as it could be the case with low carb, high in fat diets).

MORE REASONS TO EAT A MEDITERRANEAN-STYLE DIET

So far, we talked about the health benefits of eating clean and whole food compared to the everyday use of processed foods and red meat.

In the long run, the Mediterranean eating pattern would help you lose weight, cleanse your system, and reduce the risk of cardiovascular diseases, cancers, and other illnesses.

Mediterranean diet is rich in vegetables, fruits, seeds and nuts, fish, and legumes. A diet loaded of these foods is a great way to provide your body with healthy nutrients.

This diet is a very popular option for weight loss, but even if you don't want to slim, you can switch to this diet because of its health benefits.

We are all exposed to risks of health issues such as heart and cardiovascular problems, skin issues, diabetes, or even cancer. By following this diet Mediterranean diet, you are reducing the risk of these illnesses for at least twenty-five percent.

Weight Loss

This diet is a regular way of eating for people who live around the Mediterranean (Spain, France, Italy, Greece, Cyprus). These people eat foods that are locally grown (fruits, vegetables, herbs). The easy weight loss lies in the fact that the diet is focused on consuming fresh and whole-food without extra additives that only add flavor and increase your cravings. The purging effect of fruits and vegetables, nuts, and healthy fats such as olive oils helps in cleansing your body from fats and cholesterol. You are becoming healthier while losing weight. Also, this diet is an excellent way to maintain your weight in the long run. If your goal is a significant weight loss, you can combine the diet with calorie restriction and exercises of your choice.

Hydration is crucial for every diet, so you should not forget your eight glasses of water per day. The good thing here is that you would hydrate yourself through fruits and vegetables as well.

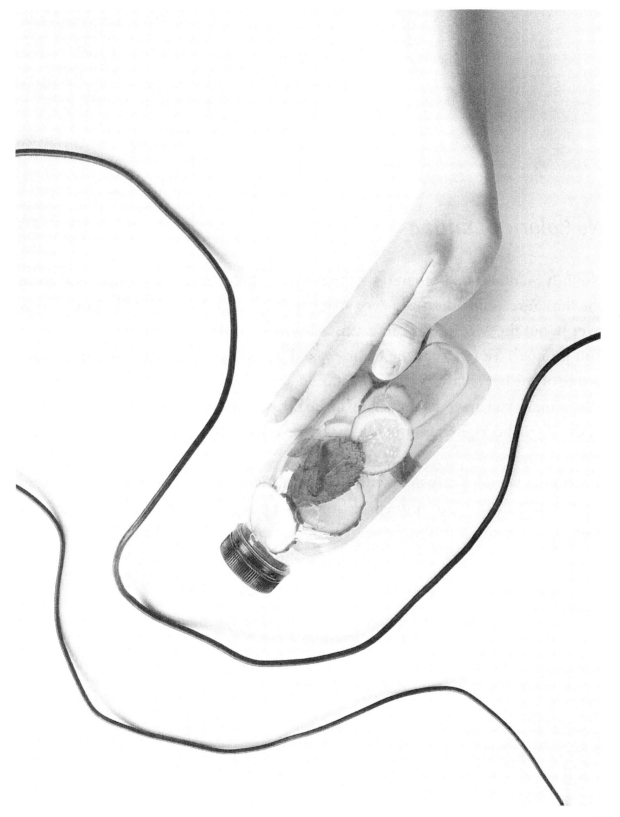

No Calorie Counting

Nobody wants to be bothered by the number of calories they consume during the day. Sure, some diets are very strict about this and would make you obsess over it, but the Mediterranean eating pattern is entirely free of this.

You do not have to count the calories, and in fact, you can eat a full plate. This is one of the best reasons why you should start this eating pattern.

Every meal you have is abundant in healthy nutrients, and you provide your body with the right amount of carbs, healthy fats, vitamins, minerals, and natural sugars.

Your body would easily deal with digestion. Even snacks are not forbidden, so next time you feel like munching something between lunch and dinner, you could freely grab a handful of hazelnuts, pumpkin seeds, or Brazilian nuts.

Fresh Food All The Way

When following this eating pattern, you know that what you buy grocery for this day or week, it must be eaten right ahead. You won't have to deal with freezing foods, forgetting about them, or eating them when they have lost their flavors. Not only will you always know that you consume fresh food, but you would actually save money.

If you have the conditions, you can always plant some vegetables such as cherry tomatoes or herbs like basil, rosemary, parsley, or cilantro.

Think of all the foods that you used to throw in the trash can, just because you have forgotten them in the freezer.

Now your menu requires you to use all your fruits and vegetables within a reasonable time. At the beginning, make sure you buy reasonable amounts of fresh ingredients (not more than you can actually consume within your first week).

The Menu Is Incredibly Abundant

Restrain a person from some foods, and they would crave it until they break their diet. I am not a fan of diets that forbid me to eat bread and pasta. The Mediterranean eating pattern is encouraging you to stay full while eating good and tasty foods. Do you want some bread? Sure, you can have some, just make sure it is made of whole grains. Do you feel like indulging in some well-cooked pasta combined with seafood? Go ahead, enjoy your meal.

You feel like treating yourself with some red meat at the end of the week (after you had a fish or seafood two or three times this week). You are allowed to eat it without hesitation.

Nothing is forbidden. Even the junk food that we all find tasty is not off the menu. It is only reserved for every once in a while.

Wine in moderation is another great option. Unlike other diets that forbid alcohol entirely, this diet has wine on the menu. You are not recommended to have mixed drinks or brandies since they contain high amounts of sugar.

In this diet there are no "cheat days", but days when you can relax and eat whatever you want. That is because even if you have a slice of pizza or a hamburger and fries, it would mean nothing if your Mediterranean-based meals are on your table every day.

You Do Not Have To Be A Master Chef To Cook These Meals

Not everyone is a fan of spending time in the kitchen preparing complex meals that take hours before they are ready for eating.

Most Mediterranean meals do not require special cooking skills. Most of these meals do not take more than half an hour (an hour max) for preparation.

These meals are ideal for people who feel like cutting some cheese, add nuts and olives on a plate. This is how the Greeks enjoy their apéritif with the so-called mezze. Often these plates include other goodies such as fruits like grape or vegetables such as tomatoes, peppers, chickpea, and so on. Splash some herbs and olive oil on top, and you would not notice when the plate got empty.

We all know how easy it is to cook some pasta. Add tomatoes, olive oil, salt, and herbs in a pot, cook it for a while and voila – there is your pasta sauce.

Fish and seafood don't require too long cooking as well, especially if you use your oven (baked salmon takes no longer than half an hour).

Mindfulness

Mindfulness means that you are aware of the present moment. Everything that you think, say or do right now is observed by your full attention. Your mind is not somewhere else, but here, focused on your work, conversation, thoughts, and even food.

We all tend to have our phones at the table and scroll through our social media while we check the latest posts. We barely notice the flavors we eat, let alone how much we ate.

A lot of people would say that they do not want to be bored while eating, but by putting your phone down and actually enjoying the meal, savoring every bite, you show yourself a form of self-love.

Enjoying the taste and paying attention to what you eat would help you eat less, chew your food properly, and feel full after you finish your plate.

Add to this, the fact that the Mediterranean diet is meant to be enjoyed with friends and family, while sitting down and slowly consuming your food, and you will realize why it is so popular.

It connects people, it helps them bond, pay attention to each other, relax, and enjoy their food and drinks.

Good For Your Budget

Healthy eating should not be expensive.

As mentioned earlier, this diet is based on the old rural ways of eating. People used to grow their food; back in the days buying food was an expensive practice, so people were doing their best to feed themselves with the things they already had – fruits, vegetables, flour, water, and fish. Meat (especially red meat such as pork, beef, and even poultry) was quite expensive and was eaten very rarely, mainly for religious holidays when people wanted to treat themselves.

Without even knowing, Mediterranean people created one of the healthiest eating habits that expanded their lifespan, kept their weight balanced, and their health in excellent chape.

Understandable, not all of us could plant a little garden and grow their fruits and vegetables, but buying seasonal fruits and veggies should not be a pricey practice.

In fact, buying your Mediterranean foods on weekly basis could save you a lot of money on the long run. You perhaps wonder how? The fact that you are now dedicated to cooking your own meals at home means that you would stop spending big money on eating in restaurants.

Also, this diet is good for the environment. It cuts the greenhouse gas emissions, reduces river, water, and land pollution (which is not the case with industries that make processed foods and meat).

INSTANT POT AND HOW IT WORKS?

You are at a point in life when you know you need to make some healthy choices, especially when it comes to your choice of food. The only problem is you can't seem to spare any minute to cook a nice and healthy meal when you get back home from work. The result? Takeout that you are genuinely so fed up of taking, but the mere thought of fighting with pans and pots in your kitchen is almost unfathomable after a long and tedious day at work.

Well, this is where our Instant Pot Recipes come in. This book is here to show you that it is actually possible for you to make the healthiest meals for your family without breaking a sweat. It's as easy as combining all the ingredients of your meal in your instant pot and in a snap, you have a hot and tasty dish ready and waiting.

The basic Instant Pot comes with the unit itself, a lid, an interior pot, a plastic piece to collect condensation, a trivet, and utensils. Assembling the unit is very intuitive; you plug in the power cord, place the interior pot into the Instant Pot, place the lid on top, and you are good to go. You will find the spot for the condensation collector to slide into place on the back of the Instant Pot, near the base. In general, you will not see much condensation collect back here; it is only for heavy flow scenarios.

The lid of the Instant Pot warrants a closer look as you will frequently be dealing with the steamer function, which will, in turn, require caution as the steam will easily heat up enough to cause burns that may not be serious but will certainly be painful. To lock the lid, you should move the steam release handle into the sealing position.

The top of the lid also features a float valve that pushes up from the underside of the lid. This valve will be down when the Instant Pot is not at a maximum pressure, which serves as a visual indicator as to if it is safe to open or not.

Under the lid, you will see where the float valve connects, along with the exhaust valve, which is covered to keep it working properly.

You will want to practice removing the covering of the exhaust valve before you use the Instant Pot to ensure you know what you are doing before it needs cleaning.

Regular cleaning of the exhaust valve is key to ensuring your Instant Pot remains at peak functionality. Occasionally, you will also need to clean the float valve, to do so you will need to remove the silicone covering beforehand; it should come off easily as long as it is cleaned regularly.

The inside of the lid also features a sealing ring, which sits on a metal rack that can also be removed for cleaning purposes. It is important to be extremely careful with this sealing ring as if it is stretched or altered in any way, it will be impossible for the Instant Pot to generate a reliable seal, severely limiting its versatility. The lid can also be propped open by simply inserting one of the fins into the notch in the handle on the base of the Instant Pot.

To close the Instant Pot securely, all you need to do is to place the lid on the unit so the arrows on the cooker and the arrows on the lid line up. Turning the lid will then align the arrow on the lid with the closed lock picture on the base. This will require a clockwise movement and will be accompanied by a chime if the unit is plugged in. Opening the Instant Pot requires a counter-clockwise movement and will also be accompanied by a chime if the unit is plugged in.

Basics on Functions

The great thing about an Instant Pot is that it is precisely designed with buttons for specific functions that will help cook your food better. The sensors associated with the buttons know exactly how hot a specific food should be and will help to prevent the food from overcooking or burning- but you still control the time, so don't leave it all to the Instant Pot.

Some of the wonderful cooking and safety features that you need to understand to make cooking with the pot easy for you include the following:

Keep Warm/Cancel

This cancels any program that has been previously set, putting the cooker in standby. When the cooker is in this standby mode, pressing this key will set forth the keep warm program, which can last as long as 100 hours.

Soup

This setting is used to make a variety of broths and soups. The default is set at 30 minutes of high pressure, although this can be adjusted using the ADJUST or plus and minus buttons.

Porridge

This is for making oatmeal or porridge with various types of grains. The default here is high pressure for 20 minutes. Make sure you DON'T use quick release for this setting as it will result in a major mess.

Note: Only use this setting with the pressure valve set to SEALING.

Rice

This is the setting which turns your Instant Pot into a rice cooker. It's an amazing program for cooking either parboiled or regular rice. For excellent results, use the provided water measurements inside the pot and the rice measuring cup. The default for this setting is automatic and cooks rice at low pressure.

For instance, the manual indicates that the cooking duration for the rice changes automatically depending on the food content. Cooking 2 cups of rice will take approximately 12 minutes, and more cups will take more time accordingly.

When working pressure is reached, the pressure keeping time will be shown, but the total cooking time is not displayed. On this setting, the 'ADJUST' key has no effect whatsoever.

Multigrain

This setting is used to cook a mixture of grains such as brown rice, mung beans, wild rice, etc. The set default for this setting is 40 minutes of high pressure while the 'LESS' setting is 20 minutes of cooking time while the 'MORE' setting involves 45 minutes of just warm water soaking, which is followed by 60 minutes of cooking time on high pressure.

Steam

This setting is used for steaming seafood, veggies, or reheating foods. You should not NPR on this setting as you will be likely to overcook your food. The default here is 10 minutes of high-pressure cooking. You will require about 1 to 2 cups for steaming and make sure you use a basket or a steamer rack as this setting can burn food, which is in direct contact with the pot.

Manual

This button allows you to manually set your own pressure and cooking time (the maximum time is 240 minutes). This button is best used when you have a recipe indicating that you should cook on high pressure for a specified number of minutes.

Sauté

This setting is for open lid browning, sautéing, or simmering.
For regular browning: 'Normal'- 160 degrees C (320 degrees F)
For darker browning: 'More'- 170 degrees C (338 degrees F)
For light browning: 'Less'- 105 degrees C (221 degrees F)

Slow Cook

This setting converts your Instant Pot into a slow cooker, which can run to up to 40 hours- but the default is Normal heat for 4 hours of cook time.

Yogurt

There are 3 programs on this setting: make yogurt, making Jiu Niang (fermented rice), and pasteurizing milk. The default of this setting is 8 hours of incubation. To pasteurize milk, adjust to 'More' and to ferment rice or proof bread, adjust to 'Less.'

Timer (For Delayed Cooking)

Usually, many people confuse this setting with an actual cooking timer, which crushes their expectations regarding the cooker.

To use this setting the right way:

Start off by selecting your cooking program (e.g., 'Steam' or any other function except the 'Yogurt' and 'Sauté') and then press on the timer button. Use the '+' and '-' for setting the delayed hours. Press on the timer setting again to change the minutes.

The time that you have set is the delayed time before the program begins. This is where you can set the pot to start cooking a few hours before you get home or wake up so that you find freshly cooked dinner, lunch, or breakfast. You should allow for both sufficient cooking time and cooking down time before serving.

With that understanding of the basics, i.e., an understanding of the functions and abbreviations, we will now move on to getting rid of any confusion that you might have while using the Instant Pot and how to avoid it the common mistakes and pitfalls of owning this helpful device.

BREAKFAST RECIPES

INSTANT POT APPLE CRANBERRY OATS

 Cooking Difficulty: 2/10	Cooking Time: 12 minutes	Servings: 6

NUTRITIONAL INFORMATION
Calories: 383; Fat: 18.1g; Carbs: 43.3g; Protein: 7.5g

INGREDIENTS

- 2 c. oats
- 2 tbsps. vegan butter
- 3 c. almond milk
- 3 c. water
- 3 apples, peeled and diced
- 1½ c. cranberries
- ¼ tsp. salt
- ½ tsp. cinnamon
- 1 tbsp. lemon juice
- 2 tsp. vanilla extract

STEP 1

In a bowl, soak the maple syrup with vanilla extract for about an hour.

STEP 2

In your IP, set in your butter to SAUTÉ. Add the oats and fry for about a minute.

STEP 3

Add the water, whole milk, followed by almond milk, and give it a stir. Add the maple syrup mixture and stir again.

STEP 4

Sprinkle with the cinnamon powder and salt and close the lid.

STEP 5

Choose MANUAL, and cook at high pressure for 10 minutes.

STEP 6

When the cooking is complete, do a natural pressure release.

STEP 7

Open the lid, and add the lemon juice and gently mix.

STEP 8

Garnish with diced apples and cranberries and serve.

ALMONDS AND OATS

INGREDIENTS

- 1 c. steel cut oats
- 2 c. coconut milk
- 1½ c. water
- 1 tbsp. vegan butter
- ¼ c. sliced almonds
- ¼ c. chocolate chips
- ¼ tsp. salt
- 1 tsp. cinnamon
- 1 tsp. nutmeg

STEP 1
Set your Instant Pot to SAUTÉ and melt the butter in the pot.

STEP 2
Add the oats for 2 minutes, stirring occasionally.

STEP 3
Add the coconut milk, water, salt, cinnamon, and nutmeg.

STEP 4
Close the lid, choose MANUAL, and cook at high pressure for 10 minutes.

STEP 5
When the cooking is complete, do a natural pressure release for 10 minutes. Quick release the remaining pressure.

STEP 6
Carefully remove the lid and give everything a stir. Let it sit for 5 more minutes so the oats can thicken.

STEP 7
Add chocolate and almonds to the top and serve.

 Cooking Difficulty: 2/10	Cooking Time: 27 minutes	Servings: 5

NUTRITIONAL INFORMATION
Calories: 379; Fat: 31.3 g; Carbs: 18 g; Protein: 6.1 g

CREAMY COCONUT OATS

INGREDIENTS

- ½ c. coconut flakes, unsweetened
- 1 c. steel cut oats
- 1 c. coconut milk + more for topping
- 2 c. water
- sea salt
- ½ tsp. ground cinnamon

STEP 1
Add the coconut flakes to the Instant Pot and select SAUTÉ. Cook for 2–3 minutes, stirring frequently, until lightly brown. Remove half of the coconut to set aside.

STEP 2
Add in oats, toasting until fragrant.

STEP 3
Add the coconut milk, reserving some for topping. Stir in the rest of the ingredients. Mix to combine well.

STEP 4
Close the lid and cook at high pressure for 2 minutes.

STEP 5
When cooking is complete, do a natural pressure release.

STEP 6
Serve warm drizzled with coconut milk and toasted coconut.

Cooking Difficulty: 2/10	Cooking Time: 7 minutes	Servings: 4

NUTRITIONAL INFORMATION
Calories: 218; Fat: 12.3g; Carbs: 19.4g; Protein: 4.4g

GLUTEN FREE BUCKWHEAT PORRIDGE

Cooking Difficulty: 2/10	Cooking Time: 12 minutes	Servings: 6

INGREDIENTS

- 1 c. buckwheat groats
- 3 c. coconut milk
- 1 ripe banana, sliced
- 1 tsp. cinnamon powder
- 1 tsp. vanilla extract
- ¼ c. honey
- ¼ c. raisins
- 1 c. grated coconut
- some chopped walnuts

STEP 1
Rinse the buckwheat with water and drain. Add all the ingredients except the walnuts to the Instant Pot. Mix well.

STEP 2
Close the lid, choose MANUAL, and cook at high pressure for 10 minutes.

STEP 3
When the cooking is complete, do a natural pressure release.

STEP 4
Transfer the porridge into a large bowl.

STEP 5
Garnish with walnuts and serve.

NUTRITIONAL INFORMATION
Calories: 474; Fat: 33.8 g; Carbs: 37.9 g; Protein: 6.2 g

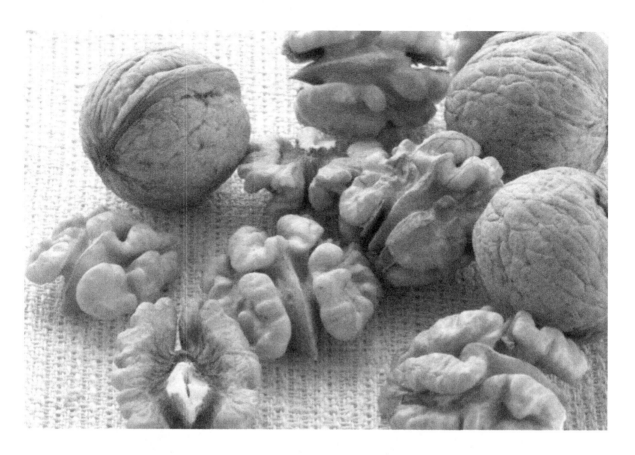

59

EGG CROISSANTS

 Cooking Difficulty: 2/10	Cooking Time: 10 minutes	Servings: 4

NUTRITIONAL INFORMATION
Calories: 482; Fat: 29.9 g; Carbs: 29.8 g; Protein: 21.0 g

INGREDIENTS

- 4 eggs
- salt
- pepper
- 5 tbsps. shredded cheddar cheese
- 1 diced green scallion
- 4 croissants

STEP 1

Place a steamer basket inside the Instant Pot and pour in 1½ cups water.

STEP 2

Whip the eggs in a bowl. Add the cheese, and scallion to the eggs. Mix well.

STEP 3

Divide the mixture into 4 muffin cups. Transfer the filled muffin cups onto the steamer basket.

STEP 4

Shut the lid and cook at high pressure for 8 minutes.

STEP 5

When the cooking is complete, wait a few minutes, and use a quick pressure release.

STEP 6

Lift the muffin cups out of the Instant Pot.

STEP 7

Slice 4 croissants in half and stuff with the muffin cup content.

SCRAMBLED TOFU ON TOAST

INGREDIENTS

- 2 tbsps. olive oil
- ½ c. onion, minced
- 1 tbsp. minced garlic
- ¼ c. diced tomatoes
- ¼ c. diced red bell pepper
- ¼ tsp. turmeric powder
- ½ c. vegetable stock
- ¼ tsp. salt
- 1/16 tsp. black pepper
- ⅛ c. minced green onions
- 2 tbsps. cashew cheese
- 2 sprigs parsley, for garnish
- 2 toasted, thick–cut bread
- 1 pack extra firm

STEP 1
Press the "saute" button of the Instant Pot. Pour olive oil. Once hot, saute onion, garlic, and tomatoes for 3 minutes or until limp.

STEP 2
Add in red bell pepper, turmeric powder, vegetable stock, salt, and black pepper.

STEP 3
Close the lid. Lock in place and make sure to seal the valve. Press the manual button and cook for 1 minute on high.

STEP 4
When the timer beeps, choose the quick pressure release. This would take 1–2 minutes. Remove the lid.

STEP 5
Add in green onions and cashew cheese. Adjust taste if needed.

STEP 6
To serve, spoon "scrambled eggs" on toasted bread. Garnish with parsley sprigs. Serve.

Cooking Difficulty: 2/10	Cooking Time: 12 minutes	Servings: 2

NUTRITIONAL INFORMATION
Calories: 144.1, Fat: 5.7g, Carbs: 11.8g, Protein: 13.9g

TROPICAL OATS WITH MANGO

 Cooking Difficulty: 2/10

 Cooking Time: 25 minutes

 Servings: 2

INGREDIENTS

- 1 tsp. coconut oil
- ¼ c. steel cut oats
- 2 c. water
- 1½ c. mashed bananas
- ½ c. cubed ripe mangoes
- 2 c. oat milk
- ½ c. chopped cashew nuts

STEP 1
Lightly grease crockpot with coconut oil.

STEP 2
Pour oats, water, and bananas into the Instant Pot. Stir mixture well.

STEP 3
Close the lid. Lock in place and make sure to seal the valve. Press the manual button and cook for 12 minutes on high.

STEP 4
When the timer beeps, choose the natural pressure release. This would take 7–10 minutes. Remove the lid.

STEP 5
To serve, divide oats into 2 bowls. Pour milk. Garnish with cashew nuts and mangoes.

NUTRITIONAL INFORMATION
Calories: 136; Fat: 2g; Carbs: 28g; Protein: 2g

SUNRISE FRITTATAS

 Cooking Difficulty: 2/10	Cooking Time: 6 minutes	Servings: 2

NUTRITIONAL INFORMATION
Calories: 196, Carbs: 4g, Protein: 12.5g, Fat: 14.9g

INGREDIENTS

- 3 eggs
- 2 tbsps. almond milk
- salt
- pepper
- ¼ c. chopped onion
- 3 silicon baking molds
- ¼ c. cheddar cheese
- ¼ c. red bell pepper, chopped

STEP 1
Add 1 cup of water to Instant Pot and place the trivet inside.

STEP 2
Now grease the silicon baking molds with oil and crack an egg into each mold.

STEP 3
Add all the vegetables, spices, and cheese on top.

STEP 4
Place the silicon baking molds over the trivet.

STEP 5
Secure the lid of instant pot and press *Manual* function key.

STEP 6
Adjust the time to 5 minutes and cook at high pressure,

STEP 7
When it beeps; release the pressure naturally and remove the lid. Remove the stuffed molds and serve immediately.

VEGETABLES

CORN CHOWDER

 Cooking Difficulty: 3/10	Cooking Time: 10 minutes	Servings: 6

INGREDIENTS

- 3 c. frozen corn
- 2 c. vegetable broth
- 3 chopped potatoes
- 1 chopped onion
- salt
- pepper
- 2 tbsps. vegan butter
- 2 c. coconut milk

STEP 1
Add the first 5 ingredients to the Instant Pot. Stir everything together.

STEP 2
Close the lid, choose MANUAL, and cook at high pressure for 7 minutes.

STEP 3
When the cooking is complete, press CANCEL and do a quick pressure release.

STEP 4
Open the lid, blend the mixture with a hand blender, until smooth.

STEP 5
Set the pot to SAUTÉ. Add the butter and milk, stir to combine. Let it simmer for 2 minutes.

STEP 6
Serve warm.

NUTRITIONAL INFORMATION
Calories: 234; Fat: 7 g; Carbs: 32.1 g; Protein: 8.8 g

MASHED CAULIFLOWER

Cooking Difficulty: 2/10	Cooking Time: 6 minutes	Servings: 4

INGREDIENTS

- 1 head cauliflower head
- 3 tbsps. melt vegetarian butter
- 1 c. water
- ¼ c. pepper
- ½ tsp. salt

STEP 1
Chop the cauliflower and place inside the steamer basket.

STEP 2
Pour the water into the Instant Pot and lower the basket.

STEP 3
Close the lid, set it to MANUAL, and cook at high pressure for 4 minutes.

STEP 4
Do a quick pressure release.

STEP 5
Mash the cauliflower with a potato masher or in a food processor and stir in the remaining ingredients.

STEP 6
Serve and enjoy!

NUTRITIONAL INFORMATION
Calories: 113; Fat: 5.9 g; Carbs: 4.1 g; Protein: 3 g

CAULIFLOWER, KALE, AND SWEET POTATO STEW

 Cooking Difficulty: 3/10	Cooking Time: 19 minutes	Servings: 2

NUTRITIONAL INFORMATION
Calories: 37, Fat: 2g, Carbs: 2g, Protein: 2g

INGREDIENTS

- 2 c. cauliflower, sliced into bite-sized florets
- 1 c. packed, fresh kale leaves, julienned
- 1 c. sweet potatoes, peeled, sliced into 2–inch thick cubes
- 1 can 15 oz. chickpeas, rinsed, drained
- ½ c. minced onions
- 1 tbsp. tomato paste
- 1 tbsp. minced garlic
- 1 can 15 oz. peeled and crushed tomatoes
- 2 c. vegetable stock
- ½ c. cubed carrots
- ¼ c. minced celery
- ½ c. cashew cheese
- ¼ c. torn basil leaves
- 1 tbsp. red pepper flakes
- 1 tsp. salt
- ¼ tsp. black pepper
- ¼ tsp. brown sugar
- 1 tbsp. olive

STEP 1
Pour oil into a crockpot. Press Sauté. Wait for oil to heat up before adding in celery, garlic, onion, and red pepper flakes. Stir–fry until onions are limp.

STEP 2
Except for cauliflower, cashew cheese, kale leaves, and tomato paste, pour remaining ingredients into crockpot. Stir.

STEP 3
Close the lid. Lock in place and make sure to seal the valve. Press the "pressure" button and cook for 15 minutes on high.

STEP 4
When the timer beeps, choose the quick pressure release. This would take 1–2 minutes. Remove the lid.

STEP 5
Turn off the pressure cooker. Carefully remove the lid.

STEP 6
Add in cauliflower florets. Cover. Press Sauté once more and cook a dish for another 3 minutes, or until cauliflower is fork–tender. Turn off a machine.

STEP 7
Stir in remaining ingredients. Taste. Adjust seasoning if needed. Ladle stew into bowls. Slightly cool before serving.

BEET SALAD

STEP 1
Arrange the trivet in the Instant Pot. Add 1 cup of water in the Instant Pot.

STEP 2
Place the beets on top of trivet in a single layer.

STEP 3
Secure the lid and cook at high pressure for 20 minutes.

STEP 4
When the cooking is complete, do a quick pressure release.

STEP 5
Remove the inner pot and rinse the beet under running cold water.

STEP 6
Cut the beets in desired size slices and transfer into a salad bowl.

STEP 7
Add spinach and drizzle with vinegar.

STEP 8
In a bowl, add all dressing ingredients and beat until well combined.

STEP 9
Pour dressing over beets mixture and gently toss to coat well.

STEP 10
Serve with the topping of cheese.

 Cooking Difficulty: 2/10	Cooking Time: 25 minutes	Servings: 4

INGREDIENTS

- 8 trimmed beets
- 4 c. fresh baby spinach
- 2 tbsps. balsamic vinegar
- 2 tbsps. tofu cheese
for dressing:
- 4 tbsps. capers

- 1 minced garlic clove
- 2 tbsps. freshly minced parsley
- 2 tbsps. extra-virgin olive oil
- salt
- pepper

NUTRITIONAL INFORMATION

Calories: 174; Fat: 8.6g; Carbs: 17.3 g; Protein: 5.3 g

BRUSSELS SPROUT SALAD

 Cooking Difficulty: 1/10

 Cooking Time: 5 minutes

 Servings: 4

INGREDIENTS

- 1 lb. brussels sprouts, trimmed and halved
- 1 c. pomegranate seeds
- ½ c. chopped almonds

STEP 1
Arrange the steamer basket in the bottom of the Instant Pot. Add 1 cup of the water in the Instant Pot.

STEP 2
Arrange the Brussels sprout in steamer basket.

STEP 3
Secure the lid and cook at high pressure for 4 minutes.

STEP 4
When the cooking is complete, carefully do a quick pressure release.

STEP 5
Remove the lid and transfer the Brussels sprouts onto serving plates and drizzle with the melted butter. Top with pomegranate seeds and almonds and serve.

NUTRITIONAL INFORMATION
Calories: 174; Fat: 9.2 g; Carbs: 14.1 g; Protein: 6.7 g

CAULIFLOWER BOLOGNESE WITH ZUCCHINI NOODLES

INGREDIENTS

- 1 medium head cauliflower, broken into florets
- 2 minced cloves garlic
- ½ c. diced onions
- ¾ tsp. dried basil
- red pepper flakes
- 1 tsp. dried oregano flakes
- ¼ c. vegetable broth
- 1½ cans (14 oz. each) diced tomatoes
- salt
- pepper
  for the noodles:
- 4 medium zucchinis

NUTRITIONAL INFORMATION
Calories: 211; Fat: 1.9 g; Carbs: 28.1; Protein: 14.3 g

 Cooking Difficulty: 3/10	Cooking Time: 7 minutes	Servings: 2

STEP 1
Add all the ingredients except zucchini to the Instant Pot.

STEP 2
Close the lid. Select MANUAL and cook at high pressure for 3 minutes.

STEP 3
When the cooking is complete, do a quick pressure release.

STEP 4
Meanwhile, make noodles of the zucchini using a spiralizer using blade A or a julienne peeler.

STEP 5
Mash the cauliflower with a potato masher or in a food processor.

STEP 6
Divide the noodles in 4 bowls. Place cauliflower Bolognese over it and serve.

GARLICKY BELL PEPPERS

 Cooking Difficulty: 2/10	Cooking Time: 5 minutes	Servings: 4

NUTRITIONAL INFORMATION
Calories: 149; Fat: 7.7g; Carbs: 17 g; Protein: 2.9g

INGREDIENTS

- 2 tbsps. olive oil
- 8 minced garlic cloves
- 2 jalapeño peppers, seeded and chopped
- 2 green bell peppers, seeded and chopped
- 2 red bell peppers, seeded and chopped
- 2 yellow bell peppers, seeded and chopped
- 2 orange bell pepper, seeded and chopped
- salt
- pepper
- ½ c. water
- 2 tbsps. fresh lemon juice

STEP 1
Place the oil in the Instant Pot and select SAUTÉ. Add the garlic and jalapeño and cook for 1 minute.

STEP 2
Press CANCEL and stir in remaining ingredients, except lemon juice.

STEP 3
Secure the lid and cook at high pressure for 2 minutes.

STEP 4
When the cooking is complete, use a quick pressure release.

STEP 5
Remove the lid and select SAUTÉ.

STEP 6
Stir in lemon juice and cook for 1–2 minutes.

STEP 7
Press CANCEL and serve.

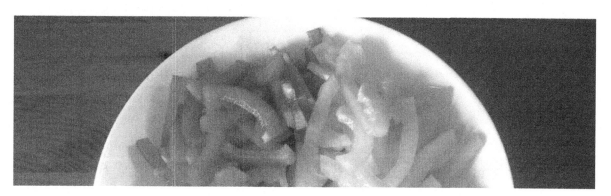

SPICED OKRA

 Cooking Difficulty: 3/10

 Cooking Time: 8 minutes

 Servings: 4

INGREDIENTS

- 2 tbsps. olive oil
- 6 chopped garlic cloves
- 1 tsp. cumin seeds
- 2 sliced onions
- 2 chopped tomatoes
- 2 lbs. okra, cut into 1-inch pieces
- ½ c. vegetable broth
- 1 tsp. ground coriander
- ½ tsp. red chili powder
- ½ tsp. ground turmeric
- salt
- pepper

STEP 1
Place the oil in the Instant Pot and select SAUTÉ. Add the garlic and cumin seeds and cook for 1 minute.

STEP 2
Add the onion and cook for 4 minutes.

STEP 3
Add the remaining ingredients and cook for 1 more minute.

STEP 4
Press CANCEL and stir well.

STEP 5
Secure the lid and cook at high pressure for 2 minutes.

STEP 6
When the cooking is complete, do a quick pressure release. Serve hot. .

NUTRITIONAL INFORMATION
Calories: 195; Fat: 7.8 g; Carbs: 17 g; Protein: 6 g

CABBAGE WITH CARROT

INGREDIENTS

- 2 tbsps. coconut oil
- 2 sliced onions
- salt
- 2 chopped garlic cloves
- 1 jalapeño pepper, seeded and chopped
- 1 tbsp. mild curry powder
- 1 head cabbage, shredded
- 2 carrots, peeled and sliced
- ½ c. desiccated unsweetened coconut
- 2 tbsps. fresh lemon juice
- 1 c. water

NUTRITIONAL INFORMATION
Calories: 185; Fat: 10.7g; Carbs: 13.6g; Protein: 4.3g

Cooking Difficulty: 4/10	Cooking Time: 30 minutes	Servings: 4

STEP 1
Place the coconut oil in the Instant Pot and select SAUTÉ. Add the onion and salt and cook for 4 minutes.

STEP 2
Add the garlic, jalapeño and curry powder and cook for 1 minute.
Press CANCEL and stir in remaining ingredients.

STEP 3
Press CANCEL and stir in remaining ingredients.

STEP 4
Secure the lid and cook at high pressure for 5 minutes.

STEP 5
When the cooking is complete, do a natural pressure release for 5 minutes. Quick release the remaining pressure.

STEP 6
Serve warm.

GARLIC MASHED POTATOES

INGREDIENTS

- 4 russet potatoes
- 1 c. vegetable broth
- 6 minced garlic cloves
- 4 tbsps. chopped parsley
- salt
- ½ c. low-fat milk

STEP 1
Cut the potatoes in medium-sized chunks.

STEP 2
Put the chunks into the Instant Pot along with the garlic and broth.

STEP 3
Close the lid and cook at high pressure for 5 minutes.

STEP 4
When the cooking is complete, do a natural pressure release.

STEP 5
Open the lid carefully and with a handheld masher, mash the potato.

STEP 6
Add milk, parsley, and salt and stir well to combine.

STEP 7
Serve hot.

 Cooking Difficulty: 2/10	Cooking Time: 7 minutes	Servings: 4

NUTRITIONAL INFORMATION
Calories: 177; Fat: 0.9 g; Carbs: 31.6 g; Protein: 6.2 g

EGGPLANT ITALIANO

 Cooking Difficulty: 2/10	Cooking Time: 5 minutes	Servings: 8

NUTRITIONAL INFORMATION
Calories: 127; Fat: 5.8 g; Carbs: 11.6; Protein: 3 g

INGREDIENTS

- 2½ lbs. eggplant, cubed
- 4 celery stalks, cut into 1-inch pieces
- 2 sliced onions
- 7½ oz. canned tomato sauce
- 2 cans (16 ounce each) diced tomatoes with its juice
- 2 tbsps. olive oil, divided
- 1 c. olives pitted and halved
- 4 tbsps. balsamic vinegar
- 2 tbsps. drained capers
- 1 tbsp. maple syrup
- 2 tsps. dried basil
- salt
- pepper
- basil leaves to garnish

STEP 1
Add all the ingredients into the Instant Pot. Stir to mix well.

STEP 2
Close the lid. Select MANUAL and cook at high pressure for 4 minutes.

STEP 3
When the cooking is complete, do a quick pressure release.

STEP 4
Garnish with fresh basil and serve over rice or noodles.

SAUTÉED MUSHROOMS WITH TOMATO SAUCE

Cooking Difficulty: 2/10	Cooking Time: 7 minutes	Servings: 2

INGREDIENTS

- 20 oz. white mushrooms
- 2 crushed garlic cloves
- 5 tbsps. water
- 3 tbsps. tomato paste
- 1 tsp. dried oregano
- 1 tsp. salt
- ¼ tsp. pepper
- ¼ c. olive oil

STEP 1

Press the "saute" button and adjust. Add in garlic and allow to saute for 1 minute. Stir in the mushrooms and saute for 2 minutes.

STEP 2

Combine water, tomato paste, oregano, salt, and pepper.

STEP 3

Close the lid. Lock in place and make sure to seal the valve. Press the "pressure" button and cook for 2 minutes on high.

STEP 4

When the timer beeps, choose the quick pressure release. This would take 1–2 minutes. Remove the lid. Season with salt and pepper. Serve.

NUTRITIONAL INFORMATION
Calories: 39, Fat: 2g, Carbs: 4 g, Protein: 2g

QUINOA WITH MUSHROOMS AND PEPPERS

 Cooking Difficulty: 3/10	Cooking Time: 20 minutes	Servings: 8

INGREDIENTS

- 2½ c. quinoa, rinsed
- 2 chopped onions
- 20 diced button mushrooms
- 1 minced red chili
- 2 red bell peppers, sliced
- 2 sliced green bell peppers
- 4 tbsps. miso paste
- 4 tbsps. soy sauce
- 2½ c. vegetable broth
- 6 tbsps. olive oil
- salt
- 4 cloves garlic, grated and chopped
- 2 tbsps. tomato paste
- 2 tbsps. lemon juice
- a handful fresh cilantro, chopped

STEP 1

Press the SAUTÉ button. Add oil. When the oil is heated, add onion, mushroom, salt, and chili and sauté until onion turns translucent.

STEP 2

Add the quinoa along with the remaining ingredients and stir. Press CANCEL.

STEP 3

Close the lid. Select MANUAL and cook at high pressure for 5 minutes.

STEP 4

When the cooking is complete, do a natural pressure release for 10 minutes. Quick release the remaining pressure.

STEP 5

SFluff with a fork garnished with cilantro, and serve.

NUTRITIONAL INFORMATION

Calories: 348; Fat: 14.5 g; Carbs: 39.2; Protein: 11.5 g

VEGETABLE CURRY WITH TOFU

INGREDIENTS

- 32 oz. extra firm tofu, drained
- 1 tbsp. olive oil
- 2 c. eggplants, chopped
- 1 chopped onion
- 1½ c. frozen peas
- 1 large green bell pepper, sliced
- 1 sliced red bell pepper
- 2 tbsps. fresh ginger, minced
- 6 tbsps. thai green or red curry paste
- 2 cans (14.5 oz.) coconut milk
- 2 tbsps. coconut sugar or to taste
- ¾ c. vegetable broth
- 1 tsp. turmeric powder
- salt

STEP 1
To press tofu, place something heavy over the tofu for at least 30 minutes. after that, place the tofu over layers of paper towels to absorb water. Chop into bite sized pieces.

STEP 2
Set the Instant Pot to SAUTÉ. Add oil and tofu and cook until golden brown. Press CANCEL and set the tofu aside.

STEP 3
Add the rest ingredients to the pot and mix.

STEP 4
Close the lid. Select MANUAL and cook at high pressure for 4 minutes.

STEP 5
When the cooking is complete, do a quick pressure release.

STEP 6
Open the lid, add tofu, and stir.

STEP 7
Serve hot over cooked quinoa or brown rice.

 Cooking Difficulty: 2/10	Cooking Time: 35 minutes	Servings: 8

NUTRITIONAL INFORMATION
Calories: 441; Fat: 36 g; Carbs: 15.2; Protein: 13.9 g

GREEN BEAN WARM SALAD

Cooking Difficulty: 3/10	Cooking Time: 17 minutes	Servings: 3

INGREDIENTS

- ½ oz. dry porcini mushrooms
- 1 lb. potatoes, peeled, cut into 1-inch chunks
- 1 lb. fresh green beans, trimmed and chopped
- ½ tsp. salt, divided
- 1 c. boiling water

STEP 1

Place mushrooms in a bowl. Pour boiling water over it. Cover and set aside for 5 minutes.

STEP 2

Add mushrooms along with the water into the Instant Pot. Place potatoes over it. Sprinkle with half the salt.

STEP 3

Place a steamer basket over the potatoes and place green beans on the steamer basket. Sprinkle the remaining salt over it.

STEP 4

Close the lid. Select MANUAL and cook at high pressure for 5 minutes.

STEP 5

When the cooking is complete, do a natural pressure release for 5 minutes. Quick release the remaining pressure.

STEP 6

Transfer the beans, potatoes, and mushrooms along with the cooked liquid into a serving bowl. Toss well.

STEP 7

Add your favorite seasonings and serve.

NUTRITIONAL INFORMATION

Calories: 169; Fat: 0.3 g; Carbs: 26.9; Protein: 6.5 g

VEGETABLE SUCCOTASH

 Cooking Difficulty: 2/10	Cooking Time: 5 minutes	Servings: 8

NUTRITIONAL INFORMATION
Calories: 114; Fat: 1.5 g; Carbs: 18.7; Protein: 5.3 g

INGREDIENTS

- 4 c. zucchini, diced
- 4 c. corn kernels
- 1 c. onion, diced
- 2 c. okra, sliced
- 6 minced cloves garlic
- 2 cans (10 oz. each) diced tomatoes in juice
- 1 c. vegetable broth
- salt
- pepper
- ½ tsp. red pepper flakes
- 4 tbsps. lemon juice
- 1 tsp. hot sauce
- 2 tbsps. freshly chopped parsley

STEP 1

Add tomatoes with juice, broth, corn, okra, zucchini, onions, garlic, salt, pepper, and red pepper flakes into the Instant Pot and mix well.

STEP 2

Close the lid. Select MANUAL and cook at high pressure for 4 minutes.

STEP 3

When the cooking is complete, do a quick pressure release.

STEP 4

Open the lid, add parsley, lemon juice, and hot sauce and mix well.

STEP 5

Serve hot.

FISH & SEAFOOD

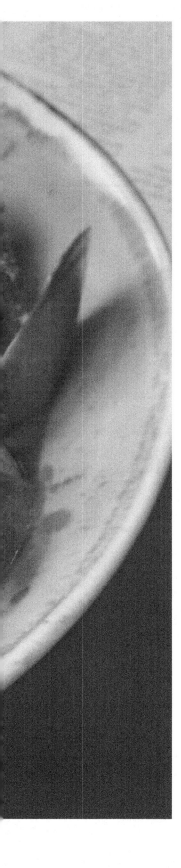

SPICED PRAWNS

 Cooking Difficulty: 4/10	Cooking Time: 35 minutes	Servings: 2

NUTRITIONAL INFORMATION
Calories: 253, Fat: 7.6g, Carbs: 23.5g, Protein: 21.4g

INGREDIENTS

- 2 lbs. prawns, uncooked, peeled
- salt
- pepper
- 2 garlic
- 1 c. fresh cilantro leaves
- juice from 1 lime
- 1 tbsp. dry white wine
- 3 tbsps. olive oil
- 2 tbsps. chili sauce
- 2 tbsps. extra virgin olive oil

STEP 1

Season prawns with salt and pepper. Set aside.

STEP 2

Meanwhile, using the Instant Pot Pressure Cooker, heat the olive oil. Cook garlic for 5 minutes or until roasted.

STEP 3

In a bowl, out together, white wine, roasted garlic, olive oil, lime, chili sauce, and cilantro. Mix well until all ingredients are well combined. Set aside.

STEP 4

Layer the prawns in the Instant Pot Pressure Cooker. Press the "pressure" button and cook prawns for 5 minutes.

STEP 5

When the timer beeps, choose the natural pressure release. This would take 10–25 minutes. Remove the lid. Serve.

FISH CURRY

INGREDIENTS

- 1 lb. sea bass/cod cut into 1-inch pieces
- 3 lime wedges
- ¼ c. freshly chopped cilantro
- 2 tsps. sriracha
- ½ tsp. white pepper
- ½ tsp. sea salt
- 1 tsp granulated garlic
- 1 tsp. ground ginger
- 1 tsp. ground turmeric
- 1 tsp. date paste
- 1 tsp. coconut aminos
- 1 tsp. fish sauce
- 1 tbsp. red curry paste
- 1 can coconut milk

STEP 1

In a large bowl add lime juice, coconut milk, red curry paste, fish sauce, date paste, garlic, Sriracha, granulated garlic, Coconut Aminos, turmeric, white pepper, sea salt and mix well. Place the sea bass/cod at the bottom of your instant pot.

STEP 2

Add the coconut milk mixture over the fish and close the pot lid. Set pot to Manual mode, on high, with a cook time of 3-minutes.

STEP 3

When the cook time is completed, release the pressure using quick-release.

STEP 4

Transfer to serving bowls and garnish with chopped cilantro. Serve warm.

 Cooking Difficulty: 3/10	Cooking Time: 5 minutes	Servings: 4

NUTRITIONAL INFORMATION
Calories: 276, Fat: 21g, Carbs: 4g, Protein: 18g

TOMATO SHRIMPS

Cooking Difficulty: 4/10	Cooking Time: 18 minutes	Servings: 5

INGREDIENTS

- ½ c. tomatoes
- 7 tbsps. tomato paste
- ¼ c. tomato juice
- 1 tbsp. cane sugar
- 1 tsp. salt
- 1 tsp. ground black pepper
- 1 tbsp. paprika
- 14 oz. shrimps
- ¼ tsp granulated garlic
- 1 white onion
- ¼ c. arugula
- 1 tsp. cilantro
- 1 tbsp. olive oil
- 4 tbsps. cream

NUTRITIONAL INFORMATION
Calories 182, Fat 6.5g, Carbs 13.19g, Protein 19g

STEP 1

Combine the tomato paste and tomato juice together.

STEP 2

Add sugar and salt.

STEP 3

Then sprinkle the liquid with the ground black pepper, granulated garlic and paprika.

STEP 4

Chop the arugula.

STEP 5

Add the arugula in the tomato liquid.

STEP 6

Pour it in the instant pot and sauté it for 10 minutes.

STEP 7

Meanwhile, peel the onion and dice it.

STEP 8

Combine the diced onion with the cilantro, olive oil, and cream

STEP 9

Then chop the tomatoes and add them to the onion mixture.

STEP 10

When the tomato liquid starts to boil – add the onion mixture and stir it well.

STEP 11

Peel the shrimps and add them in the instant pot.

STEP 12

Close the lid and cook the dish at the pressure mode for 7 minutes.

STEP 13

When the dish is done – transfer the shrimps in the serving plates.

STEP 14

Ladle the small amount of the tomato sauce from the instant pot. Serve it hot.

LEMON AND GARLIC PRAWNS

 Cooking Difficulty: 3/10

 Cooking Time: 8 minutes

 Servings: 4

INGREDIENTS

- 2 tbsps. olive oil
- 1 lb. prawns
- 2 tbsps. minced garlic
- 2/3 c. fish stock
- 2 tbsps. lemon juice
- 1 tbsp. lemon zest
- salt
- pepper

STEP 1
Melt the oil in your Instant Pot on SAUTÉ.

STEP 2
Stir in the remaining ingredients.

STEP 3
Close the lid and select the MANUAL option on the Instant Pot.

STEP 4
Cook the prawns at low pressure for 5 minutes.

STEP 5
Do a quick pressure release and serve.

NUTRITIONAL INFORMATION
236 Calories, 12.2g Fat, 3.4g Carbs, 27.1g Protein

DELICIOUS SALMON FILET

 Cooking Difficulty: 2/10

 Cooking Time: 8 minutes

 Servings: 4

INGREDIENTS

- 4 sockeye salmon fillets
- ¼ tsp. onion powder
- ¼ tsp. lemon pepper
- ½ tsp. garlic powder
- 1 tsp. dijon mustard
- ¼ tsp. salt
- 1 tbsp. lemon juice
- 2 tbsps. olive oil
- 1½ c. water

STEP 1

In a bowl, combine the mustard, lemon juice, onion powder, lemon pepper, garlic powder, salt, and olive oil. Brush the spice mixture over the salmon fillets.

STEP 2

Pour the water into the Instant Pot. Lower the trivet.

STEP 3

Place the salmon fillets on the rack and close the lid.

STEP 4

Set the Instant Pot to MANUAL and cook at low pressure for 7 minutes.

STEP 5

Release the pressure quickly. Serve and enjoy!

NUTRITIONAL INFORMATION

236 Calories, 12.2g Fat, 3.4g Carbs, 27.1g Protein

SPICY HALIBUT IN CUMIN SPICE

 Cooking Difficulty: 3/10	Cooking Time: 29 minutes	Servings: 2

NUTRITIONAL INFORMATION
Calories: 160, Fat: 4g, Carbs: 8g, Protein: 22g

INGREDIENTS

- 2 halibut steaks
- ¾ tsp. hot paprika
- 5 garlic cloves
- 1 tsp. dill weed
- 1½ tsp. ground cumin
- 1 tbsp. extra–virgin olive oil
- 1/8 tsp. salt
- ½ tsp. black pepper
- 1 lime juice, freshly squeezed

STEP 1

Put together cumin, garlic, lime juice, hot paprika, dill, salt, and pepper In a food processor. Process for 1–2 minutes or until all the ingredients are combined well.

STEP 2

Rub processed mixture into the halibut steaks. Allow the mixture to meld and be absorbed by the fish for 25 minutes.

STEP 3

After 25 minutes, layer the fish steaks into the Instant Pot Pressure Cooker. Close the lid carefully. Press the "pressure" button and cook for 5 minutes.

STEP 4

When the timer beeps, choose the quick pressure release. This would take 1–2 minutes. Remove the lid.

STEP 5

Turn off the pressure cooker. Carefully remove the lid.

STEP 6

Remove fish and transfer to a platter. Serve with cumin spice mixture on the side.

SHRIMP ZOODLES

INGREDIENTS

- 1 lb. shrimp
- 4 c. zoodles
- 1 tbsp. chopped basil
- 1 c. vegetable stock
- 2 minced garlic cloves
- 2 tbsps. olive oil
- ½ tsp. paprika
- ½ lemon

STEP 1
Set your Instant Pot to SAUTÉ and melt the olive oil in it.

STEP 2
Add garlic and cook for 1 minute.

STEP 3
Add the lemon juice and shrimp and cook for another minute.

STEP 4
Stir in the remaining ingredients and close the lid.

STEP 5
Set the Instant Pot to MANUAL and cook at low pressure for 5 minutes.

STEP 6
Do a quick pressure release.

STEP 7
Serve and enjoy!

Cooking Difficulty: 2/10	Cooking Time: 6 minutes	Servings: 4

NUTRITIONAL INFORMATION
277 Calories, 15.6g Fat, 5.9g Carbs, 27.5g Protein

TOMATO MACKEREL

 Cooking Difficulty: 2/10	Cooking Time: 8 minutes	Servings: 4

NUTRITIONAL INFORMATION
325 Calories, 24.5g Fat, 2.7g Carbs, 21.9g Protein

INGREDIENTS

- 4 mackerel fillets
- ¼ tsp. onion powder
- ¼ tsp. lemon pepper
- 1 tbsp. black olives
- ¼ tsp. granulated garlic
- ¼ tsp. salt
- 2 c. cherry tomatoes
- 1½ c. water

STEP 1
Grease a baking dish that fits inside the Instant Pot, with some cooking spray.

STEP 2
Arrange the cherry tomatoes at the bottom of the dish. Top with the mackerel fillets and sprinkle with all of the spices.

STEP 3
Pour water into Instant Pot and lower the trivet.

STEP 4
Place the baking dish on the trivet. Close the lid.

STEP 5
Set the Instant Pot to MANUAL and cook at low pressure for 7 minutes.

STEP 6
Do a quick pressure release.

STEP 7
Serve and enjoy!

LOBSTER PASTA

 Cooking Difficulty: 4/10	Cooking Time: 10 minutes	Servings: 4

NUTRITIONAL INFORMATION
276 Calories, 19.5g Fat, 5.2g Carbs, 21.3g Protein

INGREDIENTS

- 3 lobster tails
- 1 c. half & half
- 2c. water
- 1 c. shredded gruyere cheese
- 4 c. zoodles
- 1 tbsp. arrowroot
- 1 tbsp. olive oil
- 1 tbsp. worcestershire sauce
- ½ tbsp. chopped tarragon

STEP 1

Combine the water and lobster tails in your Instant Pot.

STEP 2

Close the lid and cook for 5 minutes on low pressure.

STEP 3

Do a quick pressure release and transfer the lobster to a plate. Let it cool until easy to handle. Spoon out the meat from the tails and place in a bowl.

STEP 4

Discard the cooking liquid from the pot and combine the Half & Half, arrowroot, olive oil, and Worcestershire sauce in it.

STEP 5

Set the Instant Pot to SAUTÉ and cook the sauce for 2 minutes.

STEP 6

Stir in the lobster, zoodles, and cheese.

STEP 7

Cook for 3 minutes.

STEP 8

Sprinkle with tarragon and serve.

CURRY SQUID

Cooking Difficulty: 3/10	Cooking Time: 30 minutes	Servings: 6

INGREDIENTS

- 12 oz. squid
- 1 tbsp. curry paste
- ½ c. almond milk
- 1 tsp. salt
- 1 tsp. chili flakes
- 1 tsp. oregano
- 1 tsp. ground black pepper
- 1 tsp. cilantro
- 1 tsp. curry
- ¼ c. black olives
- 1 orange
- 1 tbsp. minced garlic
- 1 tsp. dried ginger
- 4 tbsps. fish sauce

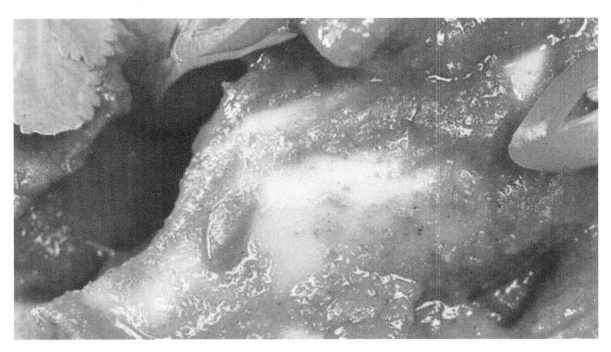

NUTRITIONAL INFORMATION
Calories 118, Fat 5.7g, Carbs 6.75g, Protein 10g

STEP 1
Wash the squid very carefully.

STEP 2
Combine the curry paste, almond milk, salt, chili flakes, oregano, ground black pepper, cilantro, curry, minced garlic, dried dill, and fish sauce.

STEP 3
Whisk the mixture.

STEP 4
Grate the orange to get the orange zest.

STEP 5
Then squeeze the orange juice into the curry paste mixture.

STEP 6
Add the orange zest.

STEP 7
Then spread the squid with the curry paste mixture and leave it for 20 minutes to marinate.

STEP 8
Put the marinated squid in the instant pot and close the lid.

STEP 9
Adjust the instant pot mode to 10 minutes.

STEP 10
When the time is over – serve the squid immediately.

SALMON WITH TOMATO SAUCE

 Cooking Difficulty: 3/10

 Cooking Time: 12 minutes

 Servings: 3

INGREDIENTS

- 6 salmon fillets
- black pepper and sea salt
- 1 tsp. dried dill
- 1 tsp. dried oregano
- 1 chopped and seeded red pepper
- 1 tbsp. coconut oil
- 1.5 c. tomatillo sauce
- 1 tbsp. apple cider vinegar
- ¼ c. freshly chopped cilantro

STEP 1
Season the fish fillets with salt, pepper, vinegar, oregano, dill and marinate for 2-hours.

STEP 2
Set your instant pot to the sauté mode, add the oil. Add fish fillets and cook for 1-minute on each side.

STEP 3
Set the pot to Manual mode, on high, with a cook time of 10-minutes.

STEP 4
When the cook time is completed, release the pressure using the quick-release.

STEP 5
Garnish with fresh chopped cilantro before serving.

NUTRITIONAL INFORMATION
Calories: 284, Fat: 11g, Carbs: 7g, Protein: 22g

FISH STEW

 Cooking Difficulty: 3/10

 Cooking Time: 12 minutes

 Servings: 6

INGREDIENTS

- 3 c. fish stock
- 1 diced onion
- 1½ c. diced cauliflower
- 1 lb. chopped white fish fillets
- 1 c. chopped broccoli
- 2 c. chopped celery stalks
- 1 sliced carrot
- 3 tbsps. tomato paste
- 1 bay leaf
- olive oil
- ¼ tsp. pepper
- ½ tsp. salt
- ¼ tsp. garlic powder

STEP 1
Set your Instant Pot to SAUTÉ and add olive oil. Add onion and carrots (if using), and cook for 3 minutes.

STEP 2
Stir in the remaining ingredients.

STEP 3
Close the lid and hit MANUAL. Cook for 4 minutes on HIGH.

STEP 4
Do a natural pressure release. Discard the bay leaf.

STEP 5
Serve and enjoy!

NUTRITIONAL INFORMATION
294 Calories, 18g Fat, 6.1g Carbs, 24.2g Protein

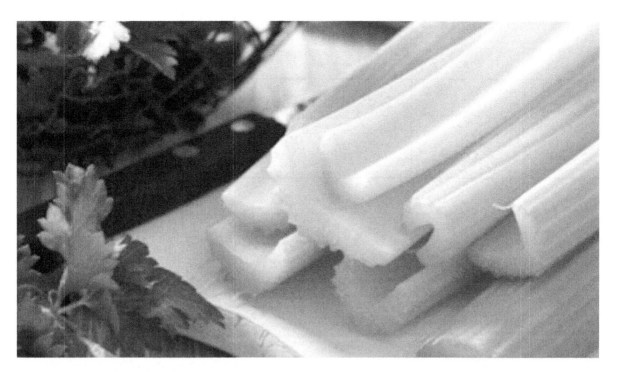

TILAPIA CURRY

 Cooking Difficulty: 3/10	Cooking Time: 7 minutes	Servings: 4

NUTRITIONAL INFORMATION
Calories: 280, Fat: 19g, Carbs: 4g, Protein: 24g

INGREDIENTS

- 1 lb. tilapia fillets cut into 2-inch pieces
- 1 tbsp. olive oil
- 1 tsp. salt
- 2 tsps. coriander powder
- ½ tsp. red chili powder
- ½ tsp. turmeric powder
- ½ sliced yellow pepper
- ½ tsp. garam masala
- 1 tsp. cumin powder
- ½ sliced onion
- 1 can coconut milk
- 10-pieces curry leaves
- 1 tbsp. ginger garlic paste
- ½ tsp. mustard seed
- ½ tsp. lime juice
- 5-mint leaves
- 3 sprigs cilantro

STEP 1

Cut up the tilapia into 2-inch pieces.

STEP 2

Slice up the peppers, onion, and set your instant pot to the sauté mode, add the oil.

STEP 3

Add the mustard seeds to pot and allow it to splutter, add garlic paste and curry leaves and sauté for 30-seconds.

STEP 4

Add the sliced-up onions and bell peppers along with spices and stir for 30-seconds.

STEP 5

Add the coconut milk and bring to a simmer. Add the tilapia along with a few sprigs of cilantro and mix well.

STEP 6

Add a few mint leaves and close the lid of pot. Set on Manual mode, on high, with a cook time of 3-minutes.

STEP 7

When the cook time is completed, release the pressure using the quick-release. Serve warm.

POULTRY RECIPES

ITALIAN CHICKEN MEATBALLS

 Cooking Difficulty: 3/10

 Cooking Time: 15 minutes

 Servings: 10

NUTRITIONAL INFORMATION
294 Calories, 16g Fats, 15g Carbs, 12g Protein

INGREDIENTS

- olive oil, 1 tsp.
- bbq sauce, ½ c.
- panko breadcrumbs, ½ c.
- salt, 1/3 tsp.
- sesame oil, ½ tbsp.
- red pepper flakes, 1 tsp.
- grated ginger, 1 tbsp.
- minced garlic cloves, 2
- egg, 1
- ground chicken, 1 lb.

STEP 1

Mix all of ingredients minus panko crumbs and BBQ sauce together.

STEP 2

Sprinkle panko crumbs over chicken and mix. Allow time for panko to soak into the mixture.

STEP 3

Form mixture into 10 balls.

STEP 4

Add oil to instant pot, place meatballs inside and press POULTRY.

STEP 5

Perform quick release of pressure.

STEP 6

Serve meatballs over cauliflower rice or quinoa drizzled with BBQ sauce.

CITRUS HERB CHICKEN

Cooking Difficulty: 3/10	Cooking Time: 35 minutes	Servings: 4

INGREDIENTS

- 2½ lbs. chicken thighs
- ½ c. water
- 2 oz. citrus marinade
- 2 tsps. minced garlic cloves
- 1 lemon
- 1 lime
- ½ tsp. salt
- ½ tsp. black pepper
- 2 tsps. cilantro leaves

NUTRITIONAL INFORMATION

194.5 Calories, 6.4 Fats, 3g Carbs, 29.2g Protein

STEP 1

Place the chicken thighs into the Instant Pot.

STEP 2

In a bowl, combine the water, black pepper, salt, citrus marinade, minced garlic, lemon and lime slices.

STEP 3

Pour the mixture over the chicken in the Instant Pot.

STEP 4

Close the lid and turn the sealing vent to "Sealing."

STEP 5

Select "Poultry" and set the cook time for 30 minutes

STEP 6

Once completed, allow the pressure to release naturally for 5 minutes.

STEP 7

Then perform a "Quick Pressure Release" by opening the valve to "venting."

STEP 8

Remove the chicken and plate.

STEP 9

Garnish with the cilantro leaves.

STEP 10

Serve.

PESTO CHICKEN PASTA

 Cooking Difficulty: 3/10

 Cooking Time: 12 minutes

 Servings: 6

INGREDIENTS

- 6 chicken breasts
- 2 c. gemelli pasta
- 8 oz pesto
- 28 oz. crushed tomatoes
- 1 c. water
- 2 c. baby spinach
- salt
- pepper
- grated parmesan cheese

STEP 1
Place the chicken, dry pasta, pesto, tomatoes, water, and baby spinach into the Instant Pot, stir to combine. Season with salt and pepper.

STEP 2
Close the lid and turn the sealing vent to "Sealing."

STEP 3
Select "Soup/Stew" or "Manually High Pressure" and set the cook time for 10 minutes.

STEP 4
Once completed, perform a "Quick Pressure Release" by opening the valve to "venting."

STEP 5
Plate the pasta and top with the grated Parmesan, if desired.

NUTRITIONAL INFORMATION
294 Calories, 18g Fat, 6.1g Carbs, 24.2g Protein

TOMATO TURKEY MEATBALLS

 Cooking Difficulty: 2/10	Cooking Time: 11 minutes	Servings: 4

NUTRITIONAL INFORMATION
350 Calories, 20.6g Fats, 6.9g Carbs, 38g Protein

INGREDIENTS

- ground turkey, 1 lb.
- diced onion, ¼
- almond flour, 1/3 c.
- grated parmesan cheese, ½ c.
- garlic powder, ½ tsp.
- chicken stock, ¼ c.
- diced tomatoes, 28 oz.
- olive oil, 1 tbsp.
- basil, ½ tsp.
- oregano, ¼ tsp.
- salt, ¼ tsp.
- pepper, ¼ tsp.

STEP 1
In a bowl, mix the turkey, onion, almond flour, and Parmesan until well combined.

STEP 2
Shape the mixture into small meatballs.

STEP 3
Place the remaining ingredients in your Instant Pot and stir to combine.

STEP 4
Place the meatballs inside.

STEP 5
Close the lid and set the Instant Pot to MANUAL. Cook on HIGH for 10 minutes.

STEP 6
Release the pressure quickly.

STEP 7
Serve and enjoy!

RED COCONUT CURRY TURKEY

 Cooking Difficulty: 3/10

 Cooking Time: 24 minutes

 Servings: 4

INGREDIENTS

- 1 lb. turkey breast fillet meatballs, 1 lb.
- 2 tomatoes
- 1 eggplant
- 2 tbsps. coconut oil
- 1 tbsp. minced garlic
- 1 tbsp. minced ginger
- 1 tbsp. minced shallots
- 2 tsps. red curry paste
- 1 c. coconut cream
- ½ c. chicken stock
- 1 tbsp. fish sauce
- lime wedges
- fresh cilantro

STEP 1

Set pot to sauté mode.

STEP 2

Heat coconut oil.

STEP 3

Add garlic, ginger, and shallots. Sautee briefly.

STEP 4

Add red curry paste and sauté until aromatic. About 2 minutes.

STEP 5

Pour coconut cream and stock into the pot. Bring to a simmer.

STEP 6

Add turkey cook on high pressure for 15 minutes. Release pressure.

STEP 7

Switch pot to sauté mode, then add tomatoes, fish sauce, cilantro, and eggplant.

STEP 8

Cover and simmer for 5-7 minutes.

STEP 9

Serve with lime wedges on the side.

NUTRITIONAL INFORMATION
382 Calories, 7g Fats, 54g Carbs, 26g Protein

CILANTRO LIME CHICKEN DRUMSTICKS

 Cooking Difficulty: 2/10

 Cooking Time: 15 minutes

 Servings: 6

INGREDIENTS

- ½ c chicken broth.
- 2 tbsps. chopped cilantro
- lime juice
- 1 tsp. salt
- 1 tsp. cayenne pepper
- 1 tsp. crushed red pepper
- 4 minced garlic cloves
- 6 chicken drumsticks
- 1 tbsp. olive oil

STEP 1
Pour olive oil into the instant pot then press SAUTE. Add drumsticks, sprinkling them with seasonings. Stir drumsticks around on each side 2 minutes.

STEP 2
Pour in chicken broth, cilantro, and lime juice. Lock lid and press HIGH PRESSURE to cook 9 minutes.

STEP 3
Perform natural release of pressure.

STEP 4
Place drumsticks on the sheet and broil 3-5 minutes until golden. Serve with cilantro!

NUTRITIONAL INFORMATION
63 Calories, 2g Fats, 3g Carbs, 8.2g Protein

ROTISSERIE CHICKEN

Cooking Difficulty: 4/10	Cooking Time: 50 minutes	Servings: 6

INGREDIENTS

- 1 whole chicken
- 3 tbsps. olive oil
- 2 tsps. paprika
- 2 tsps. onion powder
- 1 c. chicken broth
- 1 tsp. black pepper
- lemon slices

NUTRITIONAL INFORMATION
284 Calories, 18.8g Fats, 2.9g Carbs, 25.7g Protein

STEP 1

In a bowl, whisk together the paprika, olive oil, black pepper and onion powder, set aside.

STEP 2

Season chicken with the mixture.

STEP 3

Select "Sauté" setting for Instant Pot and brown the chicken breast side-down until golden, for about 5 to 7 minutes.

STEP 4

Flip and brown the other side for 3 to 5 minutes. Put the lemon slices on the chicken (optional).

STEP 5

Optional step: If you do not want the chicken to sit in the liquids, you can remove the chicken after it browns on the second side and place the trivet in the pot. Then place the chicken, breast side up, on the trivet.

STEP 6

Add the chicken broth into the Instant Pot.

STEP7

Close the lid and turn the sealing vent to "Sealing."

STEP 8

Select "Manually High Pressure" and set the cook time for 25 minutes.

STEP 9

Once completed, let the pressure release naturally for 15 minutes.

STEP 10

Then perform a "Quick Pressure Release" by opening the valve to "venting."

STEP 11

Carefully open the lid.

STEP 12

Transfer the chicken to a serving plate and serve.

BEEF & LAMB

BEEF STEW

 Cooking Difficulty: 3/10	Cooking Time: 25 minutes	Servings: 2

NUTRITIONAL INFORMATION
Calories: 209, Fat: 5.9g, Carbs: 21.7g, Protein: 16.89g

INGREDIENTS

- 2 lbs. cubed boneless beef chunk
- 1 tsp. salt
- 1/8 tsp. black pepper
- 2 minced garlic cloves
- 1 sliced onion
- 1 c. gluten-free all–purpose flour
- 1/8 tsp. cayenne pepper
- 4 stripped peppers
- 1 c. beef stock
- 3 tbsps. olive oil

STEP 1

Make a flour mixture by combining cayenne pepper, all-purpose flour, salt, and pepper. Dredge beef chunks into the mixture.

STEP 2

Put beef inside the Instant Pot Pressure Cooker. Press the "meat" button and cook beef in batches for 10 minutes.

STEP 3

Remove cooked beef and set aside.

STEP 4

Press the "saute" button and cook garlic and onions for 3 minutes or until aromatic and translucent. Pour the stock.

STEP 5

Put back the cooked beef. Close the lid carefully. Press the "pressure" button and cook for 10 minutes.

STEP 6

Open the Instant Pot pressure cooker. Season with salt and pepper. Transfer contents to a large bowl. Serve.

BEEF MIXED VEGGIE STEW

 Cooking Difficulty: 4/10

 Cooking Time: 25 minutes

 Servings: 6

INGREDIENTS

- 3 tbsps. tomato paste
- 4 medium potatoes
- 3 diced celery stalks
- ½ tsp. ground oregano
- 2 tsps. dried parsley flakes
- 14 oz. stewed tomatoes
- 4 carrots
- 3 c. beef broth
- ½ tsp. pepper
- ½ tsp. salt
- 2 tsps. minced garlic
- 1 diced onion
- 2 lbs. lean ground beef

NUTRITIONAL INFORMATION
274 Calories, 24g Carbs, 32g Protein, 5g Fat

STEP 1
Switch on your Instant Pot and open the lid.

STEP 2
Select "Sauté" cooking mode.

STEP 3
Add the beef, garlic, and onion.

STEP 4
Cook until the beef is cooked completely and drain the oil.

STEP 5
Add the tomatoes, vegetables, beef broth, seasonings and tomato paste.

STEP 6
Close the lid and make sure to lock the lid properly and then secure the valve in the sealed position.

STEP 7
Select "Manual" cooking mode. Adjust cooking time to 4 minutes.

STEP 8
Let the ingredients cook until the timer reads zero.

STEP 9
Press "Cancel" setting and press "NPR" to release the pressure gradually in about 8-10 minutes.

STEP 10
Open the pot, serve warm!

BEEF STROGANOFF

 Cooking Difficulty: 2/10	Cooking Time: 20 minutes	Servings: 4

INGREDIENTS

- 1 tbsp. oil
- 1 tbsp. minced garlic
- 1 tsp. salt
- ½ c. diced onions
- 1 lb. beef
- 1 ½ c. chopped mushrooms
- 1 tbsp. worcestershire sauce
- ½ tsp. pepper
- ¾ c. water
- egg noodles
  finishing ingredients
- ¼ tsp. arrowroot starch
- 1/3 c. sour cream

STEP 1
Prepare the Instant Pot using the saute function. Heat the oil and toss in the garlic and onions. Stir a minute and add everything except the sour cream.

STEP 2
Secure the lid and set on high pressure for 20 minutes. Natural release.

STEP 3
Change to the sauté function and stir in the sour cream. Sprinkle in the xanthan gum slowly, stirring as it thickens.

STEP 4
Serve and enjoy with some egg noodles.

NUTRITIONAL INFORMATION
294 Calories, 18g Fat, 6.1g Carbs, 24.2g Protein

153

SAVORY BEEF AND SQUASH STEW

 Cooking Difficulty: 3/10

 Cooking Time: 45 minutes

 Servings: 2

INGREDIENTS

- 1 lb. lean ground beef
- 2 lbs. butternut squash, peeled, chopped into chunks
- 6 oz. sliced mushrooms
- 1 tbsps. olive oil
- 4 c. beef broth

- 1 diced red onion
- 2 minced garlic cloves
- 1 tsp. chopped rosemary
- 2 tsps. paprika
- 1 tsp. salt
- 1 tsp. black pepper

NUTRITIONAL INFORMATION
Calories: 245, Fat: 7g, Protein: 25g, Carbs: 15g

STEP 1

Press the Sauté button on Instant Pot. Melt the olive oil.

STEP 2

Sauté the onions, garlic for 1 minute.

STEP 3

Add ground beef, butternut squash, and mushrooms.

STEP 4

Sauté until the ground beef is no longer pink and vegetables soften.

STEP 5

Press Keep Warm/Cancel setting to stop Sauté mode.

STEP 6

Add beef stock, rosemary, paprika, salt, and black pepper. Mix well.

STEP 7

Close and seal lid. Press the Soup button. Cook on high pressure for 30 minutes.

STEP 8

After 30 minutes, Instant Pot will switch to Keep Warm.

STEP 9

Remain in Keep Warm 10 minutes.

STEP 10

When done, use Quick-Release. Open the lid with care. Stir ingredients.

STEP 11

Serve.

GRATIFYING MEATLOAF

 Cooking Difficulty: 3/10

 Cooking Time: 35 minutes

 Servings: 2

NUTRITIONAL INFORMATION
Calories: 250, Fat: 15g, Carbs: 5g, Protein: 25g

INGREDIENTS

- 3 lbs. lean ground beef
- 4 minced garlic cloves
- 1 chopped yellow onion
- 1 c. chopped mushrooms
- 3 large eggs
- ½ c. almond flour
- ¼ c. grated parmesan cheese
- ¼ c. grated mozzarella cheese
- ¼ c. chopped parsley
- 2 tbsps. sugar-free ketchup
- 2 tbsps. coconut oil
- 2 tsps. salt
- 2 tsps. black pepper
- 2 c. water

STEP 1

Cover trivet with aluminum foil.

STEP 2

In a large bowl, combine all ingredients (excluding the water) until well combined. Form into a meatloaf.

STEP 3

Pour the water in your Instant Pot. Place trivet inside.

STEP 4

Place meatloaf on a trivet.

STEP 5

Close and seal lid. Press the Manual button. Cook at High-Pressure for 25 minutes.

STEP 6

Release pressure naturally when done. Open the lid with care.

STEP 7

Allow the meatloaf to cool for 5 minutes before slicing and serve.

DESSERTS & SNACKS

CHILI ASPARAGUS

Cooking Difficulty: 2/10	Cooking Time: 128 minutes	Servings: 2

INGREDIENTS

- 1 bundle asparagus
- 1 diced red chili
- ½ tsp. cumin seeds
- 1 tbsp. fresh coriander
- 3 tbsps. olive oil
- ½ of lime juice
- salt
- pepper

NUTRITIONAL INFORMATION
Calories: 440; Fat: 74g; Carbs: 34g; Protein: 9g

STEP 1

Put together chili, lime juice, olive oil, cumin, and coriander in a mixing bowl. Mix well.

STEP 2

Transfer the mixture into a cling film and roll. Put inside the refrigerator for 1–2 hours.

STEP 3

Meanwhile, place the asparagus in the Instant Pot Pressure Cooker. Drizzle in olive oil. Close the lid carefully. Press the "slow cook" button and cook for 2 hours.

STEP 4

When the timer beeps, choose the quick pressure release. This would take 1–2 minutes. Remove the lid.

STEP 5

Turn off the pressure cooker. Carefully remove the lid.

STEP 6

Transfer asparagus in a platter. Spread the chili mixture on top of the asparagus. Serve.

YOGURT MINT

Cooking Difficulty: 2/10	Cooking Time: 5 minutes	Servings: 2

INGREDIENTS

- 1 c. water
- 5 c. milk
- ¾ c. plain yogurt
- ¼ c. fresh mint
- 1 tbsp. maple syrup

STEP 1

Using the Instant Pot Pressure Cooker, add 1 c. water.

STEP 2

Press the Steam function button and adjust to 1 minute. Once done, add the milk.

STEP 3

Press the Yogurt function button and allow to boil. Add in yogurt and fresh mint. Stir well to dissolve. Pour in a glass and add maple syrup. Serve.

NUTRITIONAL INFORMATION

294 Calories, 18g Fat, 6.1g Carbs, 24.2g Protein

RASPBERRY PARFAIT

 Cooking Difficulty: 3/10	Cooking Time: 15 minutes	Servings: 2

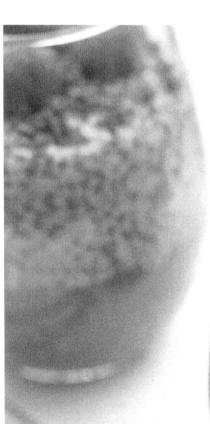 

NUTRITIONAL INFORMATION
Calories: 100, Fat: 1g, Carbs: 21g, Protein: 2g

INGREDIENTS

raspberry chia seeds
- 3 tbsps. chia seeds
- 1 c. frozen raspberries, reserve some for garnish
- ½ c. unsweetened almond milk
- ⅛ tsp. lemon juice

chocolate tapioca
- ⅛ c. seed tapioca
- 1 c. unsweetened almond milk
- 1 bar chopped dark chocolate, reserve some for garnish
- ½ tbsp. cocoa powder
- 1 c. water

STEP 1

For the raspberry chia seeds, put together raspberries, chia seeds, almond milk, and lemon juice. Mix until all ingredients are well combined. Make sure to mash berries. Cover with saran wrap. Place inside the fridge for 2 hours or until ready to use.

STEP 2

For the chocolate tapioca, put together tapioca, dark chocolate, almond milk, cocoa powder, and water.

STEP 3

Close the lid. Lock in place and make sure to seal the valve. Press the "pressure" button and cook for 8 minutes on high.

STEP 4

When the timer beeps, choose the quick pressure release. This would take 1–2 minutes. Remove the lid.

STEP 5

To serve, spoon an equal amount of chocolate tapioca in glasses. Put raspberry–chia mixture. Garnish with fresh raspberries and chocolate.

AVOCADO, BEANS, AND CORN SALAD

INGREDIENTS

For the vinaigrette
- ½ tsp. chili powder
- ¼ tbsp. minced garlic
- ¼ tsp. ground cumin
- ¼ c. balsamic vinegar
- ¼ tbsp. apple cider vinegar
- 2 tbsp. extra virgin olive oil
- ⅛ tsp. salt

For the Beans and Corn
- ¼ c. dried black beans
- ½ c. whole corn kernels
- 2 c. water
- 1 tsp. olive oil
- Salt

For the Salad
- ½ c. diced avocado
- ½ c. ripe grape tomatoes
- ¼ c. minced green onions
- Salt

NUTRITIONAL INFORMATION
Calories: 350, Fat: 2.9g, Carbs: 55g, Protein: 1g

 Cooking Difficulty: 4/10	Cooking Time: 40 minutes	Servings: 2

STEP 1

To make the vinaigrette, put together garlic, cumin, chili powder salt, olive oil, apple cider vinegar, and balsamic vinegar. Mix well. Transfer in a bottle with tight-fitting lid. Shake well. Set aside.

STEP 2

Meanwhile, pour water, dried black beans, whole corn kernels, salt, and olive oil inside the Instant Pot Pressure Cooker.

STEP 3

Close the lid. Lock in place and make sure to seal the valve. Press the "pressure" button and cook for 10 minutes on high.

STEP 4

When the timer beeps, choose the natural pressure release. This would take 10–25 minutes. Remove the lid. Let cool for 5 minutes.

STEP 5

Pour contents of the pressure cooker into a colander. Use cool water to rinse and let cool at room temperature.

STEP 5

To serve, place cooked corn and beans, and the salad ingredients in a salad bowl. Pour half of the vinaigrette. Toss gently to combine. Adjust taste as needed. Taste.

APPLE CRISP

 Cooking Difficulty: 3/10

 Cooking Time: 10 minutes

 Servings: 2

INGREDIENTS

- ⅓ c. old fashioned rolled oats
- 2 tbsps. vegan butter
- 2 tbsps. flour
- 2 tbsps. brown sugar
- ⅛ tsp. salt
- 2½ peeled apples, cored, and chopped
- 1 tsp. ground cinnamon
- ¼ tsp. ground nutmeg
- 1 c. water
- ½ tbsp. honey

NUTRITIONAL INFORMATION
Calories: 350, Fat: 2.9g, Carbs: 55g, Protein: 1g

STEP 1

In a bowl, add oats, butter, flour, brown sugar, and salt, and mix well.

STEP 2

In the bottom of Instant Pot, place apple chunks and sprinkle with cinnamon and nutmeg.

STEP 3

Top with water and honey.

STEP 4

With spoonful, drop oats mixture on top of the apples.

STEP 5

Close the lid carefully and cook for 8 minutes at high pressure.

STEP 6

When the cooking is complete, do a natural pressure release.

STEP 6

Serve warm.

RASPBERRY COMPOTE

 Cooking Difficulty: 3/10	Cooking Time: 27 minutes	Servings: 4

INGREDIENTS

- 2 c. raspberries
- 1 c. swerve
- 1 tsp. grated orange zest
- 1 tsp. vanilla extract

NUTRITIONAL INFORMATION
Calories 48, Fat 0.5g, Carbs 5g, Protein 1g

STEP 1

Plug in your instant pot and press the 'Saute' button. Add raspberries, swerve, orange zest, and vanilla extract. Stir well and pour in 1 cup of water. Cook for 5 minutes, stirring constantly.

STEP 2

Now pour in 2 more cups of water and press the 'Cancel' button. Seal the lid and set the steam release handle to the 'Sealing' position. Press the 'Manual' button and set the timer for 15 minutes on low pressure.

STEP 3

When you hear the cooker's end signal, press the 'Cancel' button and release the pressure naturally for 10-15 minutes. Move the pressure handle to the 'Venting' position to release any remaining pressure and open the lid.

STEP 4

Optionally, stir some more lemon juice and transfer to serving bowls.

STEP 5

Chill to a room temperature and refrigerate for one hour before serving.

CRYSTALLIZED SWEET POTATOES

 Cooking Difficulty: 2/10

 Cooking Time: 17 minutes

 Servings: 2

INGREDIENTS

- 2 sliced sweet potatoes
- 1 tbsp. cornstarch
- ½ c. chopped pecans
- 1 tbsp. honey
- 1 c. water
- salt
- 1 tbsp. coconut oil

STEP 1

Lightly grease the insides of the Instant Pot Pressure Cooker. Make sure to coat well so that sugar does not stick to the crockpot.

STEP 2

Put together coconut oil, sweet potatoes, water, cornstarch, honey, and salt into the pressure cooker.

STEP 3

Close the lid. Lock in place and make sure to seal the valve. Press the "pressure" button and cook for 15 minutes on high.

STEP 4

When the timer beeps, choose the quick pressure release. This would take 1–2 minutes. Remove the lid. Serve by ladling equal portions into bowls. Sprinkle pecans.

NUTRITIONAL INFORMATION
Calories: 151; Fat: 6.2g; Carbs: 117g; Protein: 7g

173

GLAZED PEARS

Cooking Difficulty: 3/10	Cooking Time: 12 minutes	Servings: 2

INGREDIENTS

- 13 oz. grape juice
- 6 oz. currant jelly
- 1 tbsp. fresh lemon
- ½ tsp. fresh lemon zest, grated
- 2 pears
- ¼ of a vanilla bean
- 2 peppercorns
- 1 rosemary sprig

NUTRITIONAL INFORMATION
Calories: 241; Fat: 0.7g; Carbs: 60.4g; Protein: 3g

STEP 1

In the bottom of Instant Pot, mix together the grape juice, jelly, lemon juice, and zest.

STEP 2

Dip each pear in juice mixture and coat evenly.

STEP 3

Wrap each pear in a piece of foil.

STEP 4

Add peppercorns, rosemary, and vanilla bean into the juice mixture.

STEP 5

Arrange a steamer basket over juice mixture.

STEP 6

Place the pears into the steamer basket.

STEP 7

Close the lid carefully and cook for 10 minutes at high pressure.

STEP 8

When done, perform a quick pressure release.

STEP 9

Transfer the pears onto a platter. Unwrap the pears and arrange in pudding bowls.

STEP 10

Top each pear with the spicy cooking liquid and serve.

CAULIFLOWER WITH ANCHOVIES SALAD

 Cooking Difficulty: 2/10	Cooking Time: 7 minutes	Servings: 2

NUTRITIONAL INFORMATION
Calories: 102, Fat: 10g, Carbs: 3g, Protein: 0g

INGREDIENTS

- 1 chopped cauliflower head
- ½ c. black olives
- ¾ c. water
- 1 garlic clove
- 1 tbsps. capers
- ¼ c. extra virgin olive oil
- ½ tsp. salt
- 1 tbsp. minced parsley

STEP 1

Pour water into the Instant Pot Pressure Cooker. Place florets into the steamer basket and place on the trivet.

STEP 2

Position the lid and lock in place. Place the Instant Pot Pressure Cooker to high heat and bring to high pressure. Press the Steam button and adjust heat to stabilize the pressure and cook for 2 minutes.

STEP 3

When the timer beeps, choose the quick pressure release. This would take 1–2 minutes. Remove the lid. Turn off the pressure cooker. Carefully remove the lid.

STEP 4

Open the pressure cooker. Rinse the cauliflower with cold water to stop the cooking process. Drain well and put in a serving bowl.

STEP 5

For the vinaigrette, in a food processor, put the oil, capers, garlic, and salt. Blend until smooth. Pour the vinaigrette into the cauliflower and toss.

STEP 6

Garnish with parsley and black olives. Serve.

TAPIOCA PUDDING

Cooking Difficulty: 3/10	Cooking Time: 15 minutes	Servings: 2

INGREDIENTS

- ½ c. tapioca pearls rinsed
- ⅓ c. brown sugar
- ½ tsp. lemon zest, grated finely
- 1¼ c. milk
- ½ c. water
- ¼ tsp. vanilla extract
- ¼ c. fresh strawberries, hulled and sliced

STEP 1

In a large heat proof bowl, add all ingredients, except strawberries, and stir to combine well.

STEP 2

Arrange a steamer basket in the pot of Instant Pot. Add 1 c. of water in the Instant Pot.

STEP 3

Place the bowl on top of the trivet.

STEP 4

Close the lid carefully and cook for 8 minutes at high pressure.

STEP 5

When done, do a quick pressure release.

STEP 6

After releasing the pressure, let the mixture stand in locked Instant Pot for about 5 minutes.

STEP 7

Remove the lid and with a fork, stir the pudding well.

STEP 8

Serve warm with the topping of strawberries.

NUTRITIONAL INFORMATION
Calories: 102, Fat: 10g, Carbs: 3g, Protein: 0g

CONCLUSION

Healthy eating is a form of self-love and self-care. Being aware of the foods you are consuming is the first step towards taking control of your health, well-being, and your state of mind.

When it comes to diets, we all believe that it is something that makes us give up on the best foods, eat less, and count calories.

But, there is this pattern of eating, commonly known as the Mediterranean diet, which is somehow one of the best options for consuming fresh and whole-food rich in healthy fats, vitamins, minerals, fiber, carbs, and proteins.

Why is this diet so potent and powerful? The simple answer is because it is an eating pattern that keeps you full while providing your body with the healthiest nutrients your body needs.

This diet offers a wide plethora of foods such as fruits, vegetables, fish, seafood, nuts, healthy fats such as olive oil, and occasionally red meat, dairy products, and eggs.

Many people are afraid that they will not be able to follow it because they are meat-eaters, but the truth is, you are not forbidden to eat meat, only substitute it with fish (at least twice a week). Red meat is on the menu as well, but not as frequently.

Based on the eating habits of Mediterranean people (Italy, Spain, France, Greece, Morocco), this diet is a popular way of eating not only for weight loss but for excellent health and long life.

This means that a piece of fruit or vegetable, fish, leafy greens, legumes, and nuts are your first choice. These foods are not packed in unhealthy ingredients like it is the case with processed foods. Your digestion would improve, and your body would be able to start burning the fats, as you are going to eat only healthy nutrients.

When eating excessive amounts of carbs, unhealthy fats, and processed foods, your body tends to use the energy of carbs and sugars first. The fats are stored as reserved, which shows around your stomach, arms, and legs.

The moment you start eating healthy foods, your body would use the energy properly and would turn to its second-best source of energy, which is the fats.

Known for its health benefits such as keeping your heart in good health, this eating pattern would help you boost your immunity, will improve your skin, hair, and nails condition, and would lower the risk of severe illnesses such as Alzheimer's, type 2 diabetes and some cancers.

Studies show that this diet works miracles for people with depression and anxiety. Foods that grow under the sun are known to improve not only your general health but your mood as well. Your serotonin levels would increase just after a few days of consuming Mediterranean meals. People love this diet because it does not require a lot of time in the kitchen and because you are allowed to eat as much as you want. There is no need for you to count calories unless you want to.

Prepare your weekly meal plan, purchase the groceries, and stick to the foods that are suitable for the Mediterranean diet. Your energy will increase, you will no longer feel lethargic, bloated, or in a bad moon. Your brain's cognitive functions and memory would also improve (this diet is known to reduce the risk in elderly people from Alzheimer's Disease and memory loss).

Your slimming would be easier, and you could keep your weight in balance in the long run.

Besides the many health benefits and the extended lifespan, the Mediterranean diet is an excellent choice for your budget and is environment friendly.

Finally, what matters is that you are healthy, content, and in a good mood.

I hope that you learned something new with this book and that it inspired you to consider the Mediterranean diet as your next eating pattern.

Eva Evans